Belgians in the Waffen-SS

Rolf Michaelis

Schiffer Military History
Atglen, PA

Book translation by David Johnston.

Book Design by Ian Robertson.

Library of Congress Control Number: 2012931453

Printed in China.
ISBN: 978-0-7643-4034-5

This book was originally published in German under the title *Belgier in der Waffen-SS* by Michaelis-Verlag.

We are interested in hearing from authors with book ideas on related topics.

Published by Schiffer Publishing Ltd.
4880 Lower Valley Road
Atglen, PA 19310
Phone: (610) 593-1777
FAX: (610) 593-2002
E-mail: Info@schifferbooks.com.
Visit our web site at: www.schifferbooks.com
Please write for a free catalog.
Try your bookstore first.

In Europe, Schiffer books are distributed by:
Bushwood Books
6 Marksbury Avenue
Kew Gardens
Surrey TW9 4JF, England
Phone: 44 (0) 20 8392-8585
FAX: 44 (0) 20 8392-9876
E-mail: Info@bushwoodbooks.co.uk.
Visit our website at: www.bushwoodbooks.co.uk

Contents

Foreword

In the years between 1940 and 1945, a total of approximately 12,500 Belgians served in the *Waffen-SS*, a number roughly equal to the strength of an infantry division in 1944.[1] Because of political and social problems and different objectives of the volunteers, however, the men were not combined in a single unit; rather, they were deployed in three different formations.

This book describes the major units of the *Waffen-SS* in which the Belgian volunteers were concentrated, where they were deployed, and the battles they took part in. It also explains the reasons why the men served in three different *Waffen-SS* divisions. In the course of this I delve into the political tensions within Belgium which still exist today.

This book cannot take into account every aspect associated with this topic. It does, however, provide in a concise manner the most important information concerning the history of the Belgian SS volunteers. The horror of the Second World War is not explicitly addressed. The reader should never forget, however, that millions of human beings were damaged physically and psychologically and that their existence suffered as a result of it.

I wish to thank all those who generously contributed to the creation of this book. In particular I would like to thank my father and Robert Möckl for editing this work.

Berlin, February 2010
Rolf Michaelis

[1] According to an SS Headquarters statistic, by 30 June 1944, 4,489 Flemings had joined the *Waffen-SS* and the Volunteer Legion "*Flandern*". By 31 January 1944 the figure was 5,033 men. From then until the end of the war an additional approximately 2,500 Flemish volunteers were recruited or transferred from other National-Socialist organizations or the armaments industry, raising the total of Flemish men who served in the *Waffen-SS* to about 7,500. As well, by 31 January 1944, 1,812 Walloons had been recruited by the *Waffen-SS* or were transferred from Wallonian Infantry Battalion 373. From then until the end of the war an additional approximately 3,000 Wallonian volunteers were recruited or transferred from other National-Socialist organizations or the armaments industry, raising the total of Flemish men who served in the *Waffen-SS* to about 5,000.

Introduction

Following the start of the campaign against Russia in the summer of 1941, Belgians were encouraged to volunteer to join the "struggle against Bolshevism". For Hitler, who wished to postpone the ultimate redrawing of various ethnographic boundaries until the war was over, this was foremost a welcome propaganda opportunity. For Flemish and Wallonian organizations in Belgium, on the other hand, having their members volunteer for military service was first and foremost a sort of advance payment which they rendered in order to have a voice in the future restructuring of their lands.

Because of the problems that existed in Belgium, however, the volunteers were assigned to one of three combat units based on their political associations.[2] Although of the roughly 12,500 Belgians only about 2,000 Flemings[3] explicitly volunteered for the *Waffen-SS* and served en masse in the 5th SS Panzer Division "*Wiking*", the history of this division is examined first. This is not just because it is before the other two units numerically, but also because the first Belgian (Flemish) volunteers joined it in 1940. Although the 10th SS Panzer Grenadier Regiment "*Westland*" was largely made up of Flemish and Dutch volunteers, the Belgians from Flanders served throughout the division. The description of the division does not, therefore, focus on the 10th SS Panzer Grenadier Regiment "*Westland*"; rather, it covers the unit in its entirety. In contrast, the other two major units (the 27th and 28th SS Volunteer Grenadier Divisions "*Langemarck*" and "*Wallonie*") were made up almost exclusively of Belgians of Flemish or Wallonian descent. For the same reasons they are the second and third to be described.

---

[2] The political discrepancies are examined more closely in the chapter "Belgium".

[3] Physical results "*k. v. SS*".

Belgium

Belgium[4] did not become an independent state until 1830. Before that, the lands that now comprise Belgium had in turn belonged to France, Austria, Spain and the Netherlands. In the 16th Century the region was part of the Spanish Netherlands of the Hapsburg Empire. Following the spread of Protestantism in the northern part of the country, at the end of the 16th Century Philipp II, Regent of Spain and the Netherlands, attempted to enforce Catholicism in Holland. He failed, and the northern part of the Spanish Netherlands (Holland) became independent. In 1792 Napoleon Bonaparte occupied the country, but in 1815 he suffered a crushing defeat at Waterloo (south of Brussels). That same year at the Congress of Vienna, the great powers of Europe decided to create the United Kingdom of the Netherlands, consisting of the southern Netherlands (present-day Belgium), the northern Netherlands, and the former Bishopric of Liège.

The protestant king William I of Orange pursued an extremely restrictive policy against the Catholics south of the United Kingdom, and a few years later the provinces of Flanders and Wallonia rebelled. This Belgian revolution led to the southern part of the country becoming independent in 1830, and Leopold von Sachsen-Coburg was crowned the first king of Belgian. Although a religious homogeneity had been created, suppression of elements of the newly-created state's population began almost immediately. The Kingdom of Belgium consisted of French-speaking Walloons (ca. 40% of the population) and Flemish- (Dutch) speaking Flemings (ca. 60% of the population). The official language was French, and in Flanders the government only allowed children to be taught in Flemish in primary school. In addition to language restrictions, the Flemings were also disadvantaged economically. These tensions still exist to some extent in the present day.

Belgium declared itself neutral when the First World War broke out; nevertheless, it was occupied by German troops and became the scene of a number of major battles. In the peace settlement after the war, Belgium was given the

---

[4] According to a census taken in 1933, approximately 8.2 million residents lived in the country, which had an area of 30,000 km^2. The country was thus roughly the size of the German province of Brandenburg.

[5] (*see* p 8) In addition to the central authorities, occupation authority was also exercised by regional and local offices throughout the country. Military government area headquarters were set up in the cities of Brussels, Hasselt, Ghent, Liege, and Mons. Beneath these were military administration headquarters and area headquarters, and in those areas where it was deemed appropriate there were also town headquarters, the lowest level.

territories of Eupen and Malmedy, adding a German language problem to the existing Wallonian-Flemish one.

Belgium again declared itself neutral when the Second World War broke out, but in May 1940 it was once again occupied by the German military. The Belgian government fled to London, while King Leopold III stayed in the country. Eupen and Malmedy were reincorporated into the German Reich in May 1940, and in June 1940 *General der Infanterie* von Falkenhausen was installed as the military commander of Belgium and northern France.[5] Not until 18 July 1944 did Hitler install a Reich Commissar for the occupied territories in Belgium and northern France (*Gauleiter* Grohé). He was to govern the country with a civilian administration more closely aligned to the Reich. As Belgium was completely liberated by Allied forces in September 1944, however, this move was more of a theoretical than a practical nature.

After the end of the Second World War until well into the 1960s, Wallonia remained the principal economic engine of Belgium on account of its heavy industries (coal and steel). Much importance was placed on close ties with France. Some political trends even favored union with France. The decline of the obsolescent Wallonian heavy industries resulted in a change throughout the nation, however. Flanders began showing a growing confidence, and at the end of the 1960s it even expelled all francophone professors and students from the Flemish University of Leuven.

The economic situation continued to change until the millennium. Wallonia was only responsible for about 25% of the national domestic product, while in Flanders the economy flourished. Disadvantaged since 1830, the Flemings had gained strength, and this new strength brought to light new political and social tensions of an economic and cultural nature. A final solution to these problems is still nowhere in sight.

Belgians in German Military Service

The surrender of the Belgian Army in May 1940 and the Belgian government's flight to London marked the beginning of hour zero for the occupied kingdom. The running of the country by a German military administration resulted in many changes in the economic and political fields. The principal beneficiaries of this upheaval were the Flemings who, unlike the Romanic Walloons, were viewed as Germanic. This was demonstrated in the summer of 1940, when the approximately 79,000 Flemish prisoners of war were released, while the roughly 65,000 Wallonian POWs remained in the German Reich until the end of the war. This distinction was also later retained in the collaborating groups and formations. Except for a brief episode in 1945, when Flemish and Wallonian SS units were combined in

"Division Group Müller", Flemings and Walloons were almost always deployed separate from one another.

The first examples of collaboration appeared in 1940, largely on account of the poor economic situation in the homeland, with the recruiting of Belgians for German heavy industry and mining. By mid-1942 the total number of Belgian workers recruited had already reached 300,000.[6]

Although the military commander in Belgium and northern France exercised legislative and executive power, in the political sector Germany also used those political groups that demonstrated a willingness to collaborate. Principally these were:

- the *Vlaamsch Nationaal Verbond* (VNV[7]) under Staf de Clerq (later Dr. Hendrik Elias). Strongly nationalist, its goal was to unite Flanders with the Netherlands.
- the *Duitsch-Vlaamsche Arbeidsgemeenschap* (DeVlag)[8]) under Jef van de Wiele. A national-Socialist organization whose aim was to incorporate Flanders into the German Reich.[9]
- the *Parti Populaire de Rex* (Catholic-Wallonian Rexists[10]) under Leon Degrelle. In the beginning at least, its objective was a clerical-fascist dictatorship under Wallonian mastery. Serious tensions later developed with the Catholic church, however.
- the *Amis du Grand Reich Allemand* (AGRA), which was created on 13 March 1941 and constituted the most powerful collaborationist organization after the Rexists. With only about 2,500 registered members, however, its political influence was almost nil.

Even though these organizations appealed to about 400,000 Belgians, including passive sympathizers, it is clear that they failed to strike a chord in the majority of the people. And so for Germany, they came to represent less a political alternative and more a source of recruitment for the armaments industry and for military and police units.

---

[6] In comparison: on 19 August 1942 more than 200,000 workers departed the Gare d'Orsay in Paris for Germany. Later there was also "forced recruitment" of labor forces in the west.

[7] The VNV was founded as a Flemish nationalist party on 8 October 1933, and shortly before the Second World War it numbered about 30,000 members; at the zenith of its existence approximately 100,000 members.

[8] For a time the DeVlag had approximately 50,000 members.

[9] There was also a DeWag (German-Wallonian working group). Led by *SS-Brigadeführer* Tittmann, its membership was only 100, and its primary purpose was to promote the interests of ethnic Germans in Wallonia.

[10] After a failed attempt to take over the leadership of the Catholic Party in Belgium, in 1936 Degrelle founded the Rex Party, whose members were called Rexists.

Recruiting poster for the *Waffen-SS* or Legion "*Flandern*".

Most of the volunteers found "fit for the SS" were sent to the SS Standarte "*Westland*" (SS-Division "*Wiking*").

In May 1940, the *Waffen-SS* began recruiting Flemings for the *SS-Standarte "Westland"* (a Standarte was equivalent to an army regiment). Its efforts were principally supported by DeVlag, from whose ranks most of the volunteers came. With a minimum service commitment of two years and extraordinarily strict entrance requirements, however, the recruiting drive met with very limited success. By September 1940, not even 50 Flemings had joined the SS-Division "*Wiking*". The number only began to climb after the war against the Soviet Union began, when the *Algemeene SS Vlaanderen*[11], which was not directly aligned with any party, lent its support to the recruitment effort.[12] By 30 June 1943, 1,853 Flemings joined the *Waffen-SS* (mainly in the SS Panzer Grenadier Division "*Wiking*"). Of these, 265 left the service when their commitments expired. By then 63 SS members had been killed, leaving a total of 1,588 Flemish SS members. As so-called "*legionnaires*", the men who had joined the Volunteer Legion "*Flandern*", formed in autumn 1941, were counted separately and are described in the following pages.

The VNV remained rather passive during the SS recruiting effort, as it viewed the objectives of the SS as a threat to Flemish independence. It did, however, recruit volunteers for the so-called *Dietse Militie* from within its own ranks. These mainly consisted of:

- the *Zwarte Brigade* (Black Brigade), whose approximately 12,000 members were organized and employed in a similar fashion to the German SA.[13]

---

[11] In September 1940 approximately 120 right-wing Flemings founded the *Allgemeene Schut Schar Vlaanderen* (General Guard Unit), which a short time later was renamed the *Algemeene Vlaamse SS*, or *Algemeene SS Vlaanderen* (General SS in Flanders). On 1 October 1942 the Flemish General SS, which had grown to two *Standarten* (regiments), was redesignated the *Germaanse SS Vlanderen* (Germanic SS in Flanders). René Lagrou—head of the Germanic SS in Flanders—vigorously promoted membership in the *Waffen-SS*. Basically unarmed, from 1943 the organization played an increasing role in (security) police actions. Elements joined the approximately 2,000-man-strong *Veiligheidskorps* (the DeVlag security corps), which operated against Belgian resistance organizations in cooperation with the German Security Police and the SD. The case of Robert Verbelen, an *SS-Obersturmführer* of the *Germanse SS* and also chief of staff of the DeVlag, who commanded the security corps, later became well known. In 1947 he was sentenced to death in absentia for allegedly murdering more than 100 civilians and resistance fighters. The sentence could not be carried out because Verbelen remained in Austria after the war and became a citizen in 1959. Verbelen was cleared in two trials in Austria (autumn 1965 and summer 1967), as it was ruled that he had followed binding orders. He died in Austria in 1990.

[12] The Flemings later formed a battalion in the SS-Regiment "*Westland*".

[13] Commanding officer was Raimond Tollenaere, who was later killed in action on the Eastern Front while serving with the Legion "*Flandern*".

- the *Motor Brigade*, which in 1943 was transferred with 3,200 men to the NSKK. In the summer of 1940 the NSKK had recruited approximately 1,400 Belgians to serve as drivers and loaders, and they were attached to the NSKK Transport Regiment Luftwaffe (active in the Brussels area). In December 1940 the unit was renamed NSKK Transport Brigade Luftwaffe. Following expansion of the units, the NSKK Group (Division) Luftwaffe was formed in January 1942. Approximately 1,000 Flemings also served in it as drivers. During the war approximately 7,000 Flemings and 6,000 Walloons served in the NSKK. Until 1942 the service commitment was one year, afterwards for the duration of the war.
- the *Wacht Brigade*, which was briefly called *Fabriek Wacht* and then, until the end of the war, the *Vlaamse Brigade*. With a strength of about 4,000 men, in July 1944 the total of four battalions were employed to form a Luftwaffe flak brigade which was directly attached to *Luftgaukommando XII* in Wiesbaden.[14]

After the recruitment of Flemish volunteers (mostly of DeVlag) for the SS-Division "*Wiking*" failed to produce satisfactory results, mainly because of the tough entrance requirements and duration of commitment, in April 1941 recruiting began for an SS Volunteer *Standarte* "*Nordwest*". With a one-year service commitment and less stringent entrance requirements, approximately 450 Flemings were recruited by the end of May 1941.

When the war against Russia began, the VNV changed its restrictive attitude towards Himmler's idea of recruiting Flemings for service in the German military. It did, however, continue to insist that the recruited members of the VNV serve in an independent national legion and not in units of the *Schutzstaffel* (SS). This resulted in the formation of the Volunteer Legion "*Flandern*", a battalion-size unit. While its title did not indicate that it was a unit of the SS, from the beginning it was administered as a volunteer unit of the *Waffen-SS*. When German core personnel repeatedly struck the wrong chord, it became perfectly clear that the propaganda about a "*European struggle against Bolshevism*" was nothing more than window dressing. In March 1942 the leader of the VNV Staf de Clerq expressed his outrage to Himmler over the treatment of the Flemish troops:

"*In the 1st Company the company commander makes no effort to hide his disdain for the Flemings. His unfair behavior is only exceeded by that of the senior NCO. The boys are harshly reprimanded for even the most minor things, and sometimes they are even beaten with sticks.*

---

[14] Commanding officer was Christiaan van Turcksin, who was born in Turcksin Peute on 27 June 1903.

[...] about 140 soldiers had been recruited from workers sent to northern France. They had been promised that they would be employed in Germany, where they would earn more money [...]

I am even more angry about the statements made about our people by officers of the Flemish Legion. In the 1st Company, for example, the Flemish are regularly called 'dirty people', 'filthy people', 'stupid people', 'gypsy people', etc. And to the Flemish officers: 'Translate that into your Russian language.' Even worse: these insults have been delivered in the presence of the population of the occupied areas. When the 1st Company was quartered in Zapol, the men of the Legion were summoned to the local square, where in the presence of 100 Latvians they were called 'gypsy people'. They were told, 'You are wrong if you thought you have come to fatten yourselves up, for you must work for your pay.' Afterwards the Latvians came to us and asked if we were really mercenaries, who are paid to fight. The boys' morale was shattered..."

The Volunteer Legion "*Flandern*" was disbanded in May 1943, and the men were integrated into the new SS Volunteer Assault Brigade "*Langemarck*" (*SS-Freiwilligen-Sturmbrigade*). As a result of this official and general transfer of the legionnaires into the *Waffen-SS*, the VNV recruited no more Eastern Front volunteers from its ranks. Nevertheless, formation of the brigade was accomplished using the 400 new recruits already received from Flanders, plus about 1,000 Flemish armaments workers. On 30 June 1943 statistics for the legion members revealed the following numbers: 2,636 Flemings had so far joined the Volunteer Legion "*Flandern*"; of these, 410 had left after their commitments expired and 266 had been killed. The unit's actual strength was thus 2,226 Flemish troops.

One year later Himmler decided to expand the SS Volunteer Assault Brigade "*Langemarck*" into a division. In doing so, he assumed that about half of the 19,000 Flemings who had fled to Germany as collaborators would join the division. In fact, only about 2,000 of these men joined the new division.

A "Flemish Guard"[15] consisting of 4,000 volunteers was formed in the spring of 1941. It was employed to guard important railway lines, canals and military installations. After the evacuation to Germany in late summer 1944, the Reich Central Security Office (*Reichssicherheitshauptamt*) also began recruiting Flemish refugees. Its focus was recruiting volunteers from the *Vlaamse Wacht* for a special purpose police battalion. The first 150 men were assembled in Fürstenburg under the command of *SS-Untersturmführer* Leysen. Recruiting ads were run in the "Flemish Post"[16] for the battalion, which was supposed to form part of a planned (Flemish) Volksgrenadier-Division. Then in January 1945 the battalion, under the command of *SS-Sturmbannführer* René Lagrou, was transferred to the 27th SS

[15] The so-called *Vlaamse Wacht* is not to be confused with the *Vlaamse Wacht Brigade*.

[16] Newspaper for Flemish refugees in Germany.

Volunteer Grenadier Division "*Langemarck*" (Flemish No. 1) in the Lüneburg Heath. There training continued, and new arrivals were integrated into the unit, which was now called SS Police Battalion "*Flandern*". The battalion saw no action. One small group did escort the politically-active Flemish priest Cyril Verschaeve to Ebensee.

The Wallonian volunteers were generally placed in separate formations to avoid a confrontation with the Flemings. The Rexists, in particular, and the AGRA recruited from within their ranks for service in various German civilian and military units. The Wallonian 373rd Infantry Battalion (Legion "*Wallonie*") consisted mainly of members of the *Parti Populaire de Rex*. Older age classes and members of the AGRA mainly provided volunteers for:

- the NSKK Group Luftwaffe (about 6,000 Wallonians).
- the Todt Organization (about 4,000 Wallonians).
- the *Garde Wallonne*, which from 1941 was used to guard railway lines and other transportation systems.

Until 1943, Himmler had no interest in Wallonian military volunteers—neither for the *Waffen-SS*, nor in the form of a legion to take part in the struggle against Bolshevism—for ideological reasons. Not until May 1943 did he change his mind. It was then that he decided to place the Walloons, now characterized as "French-speaking Germanics", in an SS Volunteer Mountain Brigade "*Wallonie*", to be part of the Germanic SS Panzer Corps then being considered. However, recruitment in Belgium only attracted about 300 volunteers between the ages of 17 and 40.

In the autumn of 1944 a plan to combine all Wallonians still interested in collaboration in the 28th SS Volunteer Grenadier Division "*Wallonien*" also failed. Few Wallonian armament workers in Germany volunteered, and the roughly 2,000 volunteers from the NSKK, the *Garde Wallonne*, etc. represented only a fraction of the personnel required.

Various Belgian volunteers served in other units of the *Waffen-SS* until the end of the war. Most were officer candidates who were assigned to another SS unit after completing officer training at an *SS-Junkerschule*. Worthy of special mention is the 38th SS Grenadier Division. The officer candidates of the just-completed 18th Wartime Officer Course and of the 4th (Germanic) Preparation Course at the *SS-Junkerschule Tölz* were assigned to the new SS division, which was only formed in April 1945, to serve as core personnel.

After the war a total of about 57,000 Belgians—mainly active collaborators—were accused of siding with Germany. 43,000 of these were deprived of their civil and political rights (such as the right to vote). Of the just under 3,000 death sentences, 242 were carried out. With a population of 8.2 million Belgians in 1933, this was equivalent to a rate of less than 1%. Of the volunteers who joined the *Waffen-SS*, the relationship to the population was just 0.14%. Even if one assumes that the number of passive national-socialist sympathizers in Belgium was somewhat higher, the general disinterest in the Greater German Reich in Europe is evident.

Belgians in the *Waffen-SS*

5th SS Panzer Division "*Wiking*"

The SS Motorized Division "*Wiking*"

On 6 September 1940, the OKW placed the number of German volunteers for the *Waffen-SS* from the 1920 age class at 15,718. Several days later Hitler ordered the formation of the **SS Motorized Division "*Germania*"**[17]. In order to achieve the division's authorized strength of approximately 20,000 men, volunteers were to be recruited from Belgium (Flanders), the Netherlands, Denmark, and Norway.

Recruitment of Danes and Norwegians for an *SS-Standarte "Nordland"* had begun at the end of April 1940 after "Operation *Weserübung*"—the occupation of Denmark and Norway. The recruitment of Flemings and Netherlanders followed from June 1940.

Apart from personnel questions, the formation of an additional motorized division led to problems even before the invasion of the Soviet Union. On 8 November 1940 the OKW war diary noted:

"*When informed by the army Commander-in-Chief that the formation of a fourth three-part motorized SS division by the spring of 1941 would delay the provision of vehicles of two of the ten new motorized divisions being formed or four twelfth wave divisions by about two months until the end of May 1941, the Führer decided that formation of the ten motorized divisions must not be delayed by the formation of the fourth SS division and that the twelfth wave divisions whose formation cannot be completed should be organized by 1 April 1941 so that they can be employed with restrictions. Sufficient new production vehicles are to be allocated to the fourth SS division to enable it to be field-usable by 1 April 1941.*"

The unit, whose composition was supposed to be 3/4 Reich Germans and 1/4 "*personnel coming from related countries (Flanders, Netherlands, Norway and Denmark)*", was also characterized as a "*Nordic division*". Following the transfer of the *SS-Standarte*[18] *"Germania"* from the *SS-Verfügungs-Division*, its organization was to be as follows:

---

[17] It was initially planned to give the *SS-Verfügungs-Division* the name of the 1st Regiment "*Deutschland*" and the new division the name of the 2nd Regiment "*Germania*".

[18] The designation *Standarte*/Regiment was in some cases used simultaneously by the various agencies.

Troops of the SS-Division (Motorized) "*Wiking*" in action in the Caucasus.

Division Headquarters		Munich
SS-Standarte "Germania"	(I-III Sturmbann)	Altomünster
SS-Standarte "Westland"	(I-III Sturmbann)	Munich
SS-Standarte "Nordland"	(I-III Sturmbann)	Vienna
SS Artillery Standarte		Dachau
SS Signals Standarte		Nuremberg
SS Reconnaissance Battalion		Munich
SS Anti-Tank Battalion		Aichach
SS Pioneer Battalion		Allershausen
SS Supply Services		Dachau
SS Medical Services		Dachau

On 21 December 1940, Hitler ordered the unit renamed the SS Motorized Division "*Wiking*". As its commander he named the former commander of the *SS-Standarte "Deutschland"*, *SS-Brigadeführer* Steiner.

The flow of "*Germanic*" volunteers remained far below expectations. Of the desired total of about 5,000 foreigners, by mid-January 1941 only about 600 Netherlanders and 100 Flemings had volunteered for the *SS-Standarte "Westland"*, plus approximately 200 Danes and 240 Norwegians for the *SS-Standarte "Nordland"*. Subsequently, on 22 February 1941 Hitler authorized the *SS-Hauptamt* (SS Headquarters) to begin recruiting Finnish volunteers. Although not of "Germanic" stock, the Finns were at least northern Europeans. About half of these men ultimately formed the III Battalion of the *SS-Standarte "Nordland"*. At the beginning of 1941, therefore, there were only slightly more than 2,000 northern and western European volunteers in the 20,000-man division.

Unit level training at Training Camp Heuberg was concluded at the end of March 1941. On 1 April 1941, the division came under the command of Army Group C. At the beginning of June 1941 the division was transported by rail into the area north of Breslau, where it was deployed as part of the XIV Motorized Army Corps, itself part of Panzer Group 1, for the coming offensive in the east. On 18 June the units moved into the area southeast of Lublin. One week after the start of "Operation Barbarossa" the unit was ordered to Lvov via Zamość. From there it marched toward Ternopol, approximately 120 km away. It was there that the unit first saw combat.

At the beginning of July 1941 fierce fighting developed during the crossing of the Sprucz River, which had previously formed the border between Poland and the Ukraine, neat Santanov and Husiatyn. Despite pouring rain and softened roads, the SS-Division "*Wiking*" reached the Bug River near Proskurov on 7 July 1941. Nine days later there were fierce battles at Tarascha. While elements of the division marched south with the XIV Motorized Army Corps to assist in the destruction of the enemy forces in the Uman pocket, on 29 July the bulk of the division was

Type 166 four-wheel-drive VW (Schwimmwagen).

Panzer III Ausf. K of the SS Panzer Battalion "*Wiking*".

attached to the III Motorized Army Corps and deployed along the Ross River toward Kanev on the Dniepr. From there the units pursued the enemy forces retreating south of the Dniepr to Smyela, during which fierce fighting developed on 6 August. Just two weeks later the division found itself 250 km farther to the east near Dnepropetrovsk. The units had covered more than 1,000 kilometers in just under two months.

Deployed in the Dnepropetrovsk bridgehead, the division took part in several extremely difficult defensive actions until 28 September 1941. At the beginning of October 1941 the units took part in the drive toward Pavlograd. The autumn rains set in, turning the roads into mud, and the division, from 10 October again under the XIV Motorized Army Corps, received almost no supplies until the end of the month. At the beginning of November Panzer Group 1 crossed the Mius and advanced on Rostov. In those days then *SS Funker* (radio operator) Hans Karl Erlewein (1st Company, *SS-Standarte "Westland"*) wrote a letter to his parents. He was still confident that "Operation Barbarossa" would be ending soon:

"At last I have time to write a few words. Things are going pretty well. My only complaint is the terrible diarrhea that everyone has. It comes from our fatty rations. We have been sitting here in a Russian village for several days. The place is completely louse-infested. I have bites all over my body and have been pricked all over by lice and bedbugs.

The Russians are retreating steadily now. We hope that this campaign will soon be over. […]

We don't mind when the Russian artillery fire becomes a little heavier, for then we know that the Russians are pulling out, which means running away as fast as they can go! Several days ago we watched a dive-bombing attack by 12 German machines on a Russian village where there were tanks and much artillery. You should have seen how the Russians skedaddled when the first one began its dive!"

After fierce fighting and a powerful Russian counterattack, Panzer Group 1 withdrew behind the Mius River and took up winter positions there. Since entering combat on 1 July 1941, the SS-Division "*Wiking*" had suffered 50% casualties through death, wounds, or freezing. The regiments took up quarters in the area north of Uspenskaya to Alexeyevka in the south. In Uspenskaya the SS Medical Battalion "*Wiking*" set up a collection point for the ambulatory care of frostbite cases.

The Soviets launched further counterattacks from 7 to 13 December and on 25 and 26 December 1941. In February 1941 the Finnish Battalion joined the division, replacing the first 400 Finnish volunteers, who returned to Finland after completing their one-year commitment. At the same time, just under 400 Norwegians also

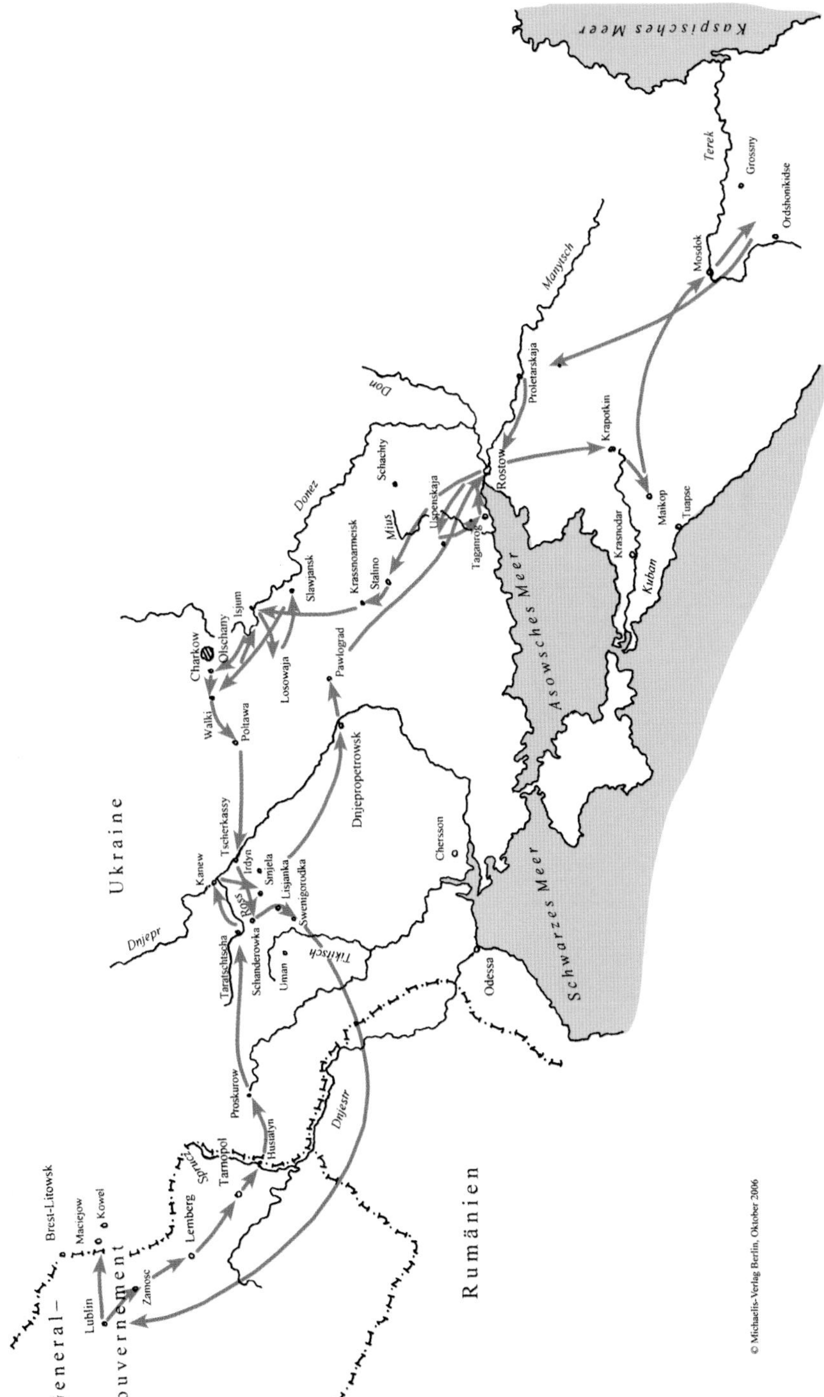

Actions by the SS-Division (Motorized) "*Wiking*" (July 1941 – May 1944).

returned home after completing their tours with the division. They had no interest in serving any longer. Because of casualties and the absence of replacements, the SS-Regiments "*Westland*" and "*Nordland*" each temporarily disbanded one battalion.

In January 1942, a battle group was formed and sent north to the hard-pressed III Panzer Corps. During their winter offensive, the Soviets had broken through the German positions in the Izyum area to a depth of 100 kilometers. After about eight weeks the men returned to the division. At the same time an SS Panzer battalion reached the unit; consequently, the division's organization was almost equivalent to that of a panzer grenadier division.

After being wounded, *SS-Funker* Hans Karl Erlewein described the unusual quiet at the front in a letter to his mother dated 27 April 1942:

"*I am finally back where I belong. We arrived at the company yesterday evening. First to greet us was the battalion commander. He immediately recognized me when I said my name. He has been promoted to SS-Sturmbannführer and has the German Cross in Gold. The journey was uneventful apart from some anti-aircraft fire. The front is still 3 km away and we're moving up this evening. Believe me, I am telling the complete truth, there's not a shot to be heard day or night. Here at the front it's just as quiet as it is for you at home and it will probably remain so for a few more weeks.*"

After more than half a year in the Mius position, on 16 July 1942 the SS-Division "*Wiking*" was relieved and moved to the LVII Panzer Corps in the area northwest of Taganrog. The attack on Rostov began five days later. On 23 July 1942 the division took the city, and soon afterwards crossed the Don heading south. By 5 August the division covered almost 250 km. There was little fighting until it reached the Kuban. The SS-Regiment "*Nordland*" was ordered to take Krapotkin and the SS-Regiment "*Germania*" Grigoripolitskaya. After assembling around Grigoripolitskaya, the SS-Division "*Wiking*" crossed the Kuban and struck out toward the Laba. On 9 August 1942 the division crossed the river in the Petroparyovskaya area and drove west. The next day the first elements of the division crossed the Belaya River near Velikoye. On 14 August 1942 the units occupied the Chadyshenskaya oil district.

As the motorized division was unable to advance across the Caucasus Mountains toward Tuapse, on the Black Sea, approximately 100 km away in a straight line, it initially halted and was reinforced by the SS-Regiment "*Westland*". Then *SS-Sturmmann* Günter Adam remembered:

"The division headquarters moved to Maykop. Again we drove past fields of melons, tomatoes, sunflowers and especially grapes. At every halt some of us stood guard while others picked fruit. We especially liked the big green watermelons. The weather was fine and dry, the temperature rose to over 30 degrees. Our mosquito nets were very uncomfortable, however, as the heat built up beneath them. Every day we took an atabrine tablet against malaria (in the summer of 1941 we still had to take quinine, which was terribly bitter, especially as we had to crush the tablets in our mouths)."

After the XXXXIV Jäger Corps moved into the front, on 19 September 1942 the SS-Division "*Wiking*" was removed from the LVIII Panzer Corps and sent via Maykop to LII Army Corps (1st Panzer Army) in the Mozdok area on the Terek River, about 350 kilometers distant.

On 27 September 1942 the division moved out of the area south of Mozdok and attacked Malgobek in order to gain a base from which to later attack Grozny. After heavy fighting, Mozdok fell on 5 October 1942.

The SS Panzer Grenadier Division "*Wiking*"

On 9 November 1942 the unit was renamed SS Panzer Grenadier Division "*Wiking*". When, to the south, the Red Army succeeded in encircling elements of the 13th Panzer Division between Ordzhonikidze and Gisel farther to the west, the "*Wiking*" Division was sent to III Panzer Corps. As the division had been formed as a motorized unit and already possessed a panzer battalion, becoming an SS panzer grenadier division did not bring about any significant organizational changes. The III (Armored) Battalion, SS Panzer Grenadier Regiment "*Germania*" was reformed in France and did not rejoin the division until 1944.

On 16 November 1942 the units began the successful relief of the 13th Panzer Division, and subsequently occupied positions west of Gisel together with army units. Following the encirclement of the 6th Army in Stalingrad on 22 November 1942, on Christmas Day 1942 the SS Panzer Grenadier Division "*Wiking*" received orders to join the 4th Panzer Army, which had been tasked with relieving the 6th Army.

After a rail and road journey of about 500 kilometers, the first elements of the division arrived in the area north of Proletarskaya (approx. 175 km east of Rostov) on 27 December 1942. Attached to LVII Panzer Corps, the division immediately became involved in fierce defensive fighting. A relief of the 6th Army was out of the question. In January 1943 the Manych River, near Proletarskaya, formed a line from which the Soviet tank attacks could be halted at least temporarily.

The Soviets eventually crossed the river, and the German forces began falling back toward Rostov. The Soviet forces advanced so rapidly that the retreat became almost a flight. On 5 February 1943 the SS Panzer Grenadier Division "*Wiking*" reached Rostov after a march of about 175 kilometers with almost constant enemy contact. There the division was released from the LVII Panzer Corps (4th Panzer Army) and sent to the III Panzer Corps (1st Panzer Army). The latter formation was supposed to stabilize the front west of the Donets from the Stalino area, approximately 180 kilometers to the northwest.

Before this could take place, however, the Red Army made further large gains toward the west, and the SS Panzer Grenadier Division "*Wiking*" was ordered into the Krasnoarmeysk area. There were fears that a Soviet drive west of Stalino might trap the entire Army Group Don to the south against the Black Sea. On 10 February 1943 fighting broke out in the Krasnoarmeysk area against elements of the Soviet 4th Guards Tank Corps. SS Panzer Grenadier Division "*Wiking*" counterattacked on 18 February 1943. Surprisingly bad Soviet command, plus fuel shortages, resulted in the destruction of the enemy tank corps in the Krasnoarmeysk – Grishino area.

Now attached to the XXXX Panzer Corps, the division took part in the German counter-operations which retook the area up to the Donets. At the beginning of March 1943 the unit took up positions between Izyum and Protopokovka on the Donets.

Men of the SS Panzer Grenadier Division "*Wiking*" in action at the Donets River (spring 1943).

Effective 18 March 1943, the SS Panzer Grenadier Regiment "*Nordland*" was removed from the SS Panzer Grenadier Division "*Wiking*", in order to form the core of a new unit, the SS Panzer Grenadier Division "*Nordland*". The III (Finnish) Battalion, SS Panzer Grenadier Regiment "*Nordland*", also left the unit to return to Finland. It was disbanded in Hanko on 11 July 1943.

In mid-April 1943, the remaining elements of the division began moving into the Losovaya area (approx. 80 km southwest of Izyum) to rest and refit. In addition to replacements from home, the division's strength was bolstered through the addition of the Estonian SS-Panzer Grenadier Battalion "*Narva*". One month later the SS-Panzer Grenadier Division "*Wiking*" was moved back into the Slavyansk area (approx. 45 km southeast of Izyum) as army reserve.

Attached to the XXIV Panzer Corps, on 5 July 1943 the division was ordered into the area north of Valki (approx. 50 km west of Kharkov). There the unit formed Army Detachment Kempf's reserve for "Operation Citadel". On 16 July 1943 the division command received orders to move back into the Izyum area. Two days later the first units to arrive there attacked a Soviet bridgehead across the Donets. Without effective support from heavy weapons the attack failed. The division was, however, able to repulse several heavy enemy attacks from the bridgehead. On 19 July 1943 SS Panzer Grenadier Battalion "*Narva*" was involved in a dramatic action after about 100 Soviet tanks overran the Estonian positions. By summoning all its forces the division was able to repulse the attack.

The Red Army shifted its focus, and at the beginning of August 1943 attacked southeast of Izyum in the direction of Slavyansk. There, too, the German forces were initially able to halt the Soviet advance after fierce fighting. Attempts to throw the enemy back beyond the Donets failed, however. Losses were heavy.

On 5 August 1943 SS Panzer Grenadier Division "*Wiking*" was pulled out of action, and on 11 August it marched back into the Kharkov area. The next day the units arrived at Olshany (approx. 20 km west of Kharkov) and were attached to the III Panzer Corps (8th Army). Fighting began the next day and climaxed on 18-19 August in fierce offensive and defensive battles. SS Panzer Grenadier Division "*Wiking*" alone destroyed 84 enemy tanks in the fighting. Given the Soviets' materiel superiority, however, the only result was a short-lived reduction in their attacks.

The Soviets resumed their offensive at the end of August 1943. The units pulled back and tired unsuccessfully to establish a new defense front near Valki (approx. 50 km west of Kharkov). After a fighting withdrawal of almost 300 km the division reached the Dniepr via Poltava, and on 27 September 1943 crossed the river near Cherkassy.

Just several days later, the Red Army was able to cross the island-dotted river in several places, establishing a number of bridgeheads, including one at the mouth of the Rossava (approx. 30 km north of Cherkassy). In fierce fighting German units, including the SS Panzer Grenadier Regiment "*Westland*", were able to at least partially drive the enemy from the west bank onto the islands in the river or completely onto the east back.

Finally, as part of XXXXII Army Corps, the SS Panzer Grenadier Division "*Wiking*" took over an approximately 50-kilometer sector of the main line of resistance between Kanev and Cherkassy. In addition to the construction of defensive positions, which in places was very difficult, the division also had to take part in frequent operations against partisans operating in the rear.

The 5th SS Panzer Division "*Wiking*"

On 22 October 1943, coincident with the numbering of *Waffen-SS* units, the division was renamed and reorganized as the **5th SS Panzer Division "*Wiking*"**. The number "5" was added to all division units and the two panzer grenadier regiments were numbered as follows:

SS Panzer Grenadier Regiment **9** "*Germania*"
SS Panzer Grenadier Regiment **10** "*Westland*"

With the formation of SS Panzer Regiment 5, the former SS Panzer Battalion "*Wiking*" became the new unit's I Battalion. At the beginning of January 1944 it had just under 30 tanks. The II Battalion, which was to be equipped with the Panzer V Panther, would not join the division until summer 1944.

On the Dniepr, the Red Army succeeded in establishing a bridgehead near Cherkassy on 13 November 1943. Reinforcements were rushed to the scene. Among the units sent to the hotly-contested area was the newly-formed 5th SS Volunteer Assault Brigade "*Wallonien*", which arrived on 20 November[19]. On 14 December Soviet units took the fiercely defended town of Cherkassy, allowing them to expand their bridgehead over the Dniepr more than 20 kilometers to Smela. The positions held by the 5th SS Panzer Division subsequently ran from south of Kanev along the Dniepr in the direction of Cherkassy, where they turned southwest in the direction of Smela.

The division's reported strength on 31 December 1943 was:

Officers	NCOs	Enlisted Men	Total
430	2,748	11,469	14,647
2.9%	18.8%	78.3%	100%

The numbers do not include the II Battalion, SS Panzer Regiment 5, which had not yet reached the front, or the III (Armored) Battalion, SS Panzer Grenadier Regiment 9 "*Germania*", then under formation. The division's combat strength was about 12,500 men, approximately 70% of authorized strength.

As a result of Hitler's order to hold the positions on the Dniepr, in the course of the Soviet offensive that began on 25 January 1944, the Red Army was able to encircle the XI and XXXXII Army Corps in the area between Zvenigorodka – Kanev – Cherkassy on 28 January.

[19] See Chapter 28: SS Volunteer Grenadier Division "*Wallonien*" (Wallonian No. 1).

Initially the 5th SS Panzer Division "*Wiking*" employed rear-echelon troops to establish thin blocking lines in the southwest part of the pocket. There was especially heavy fighting near Olshana beginning 28 January 1944. Division supply units defended the town, whose loss would have meant the splitting of the pocket. Reinforcements arrived in the form of elements of SS Armored Pioneer Battalion 5, SS Panzer Grenadier Battalion "*Narva*" and I Battalion, SS Panzer Regiment 5, and the positions were held until 5 February.

The German breakout attempt began two days later. On 9 February SS Panzer Grenadier Regiment 9 "*Germania*" received orders to advance into the enemy-held Shanderovka area. There it was supposed to be met by troops of the III Panzer Corps. On 15 February 1944 German combat units tried to fight their way through to the encircled troops from the west. Hampered by mud and Soviet resistance, the effort was futile.

On 16 February 1944, with Hitler's approval, the more than 50,000 encircled German troops launched a breakout attempt toward Lysyanka to the southwest. East of Shanderovka, the last surviving tanks of I Battalion, SS Panzer Regiment 5 covered the 57th and 88th Infantry Divisions, which made up the rearguard. Organized into battle groups, the bulk of the 5th SS Panzer Division "*Wiking*" and the attached 5th SS Volunteer Assault Brigade "*Wallonien*" formed the breakout's left, or southern, flank.

Pounded by Soviet artillery and tank fire and continuous air attack, on 17 February 1944 approximately 34,000 men reached the positions of the German III Panzer Corps on the west bank of the Gnilio Tikich. Georg Neuber remembered:

"*On 28 January 1944 the ring around the Cherkassy pocket closed. That put an end to my request for marriage leave. At about noon on 30 January 1944 I returned from the aid station, where I had been receiving ambulatory treatment for a large abscess on my left foot. When I arrived at my radio post I was ordered to report to the senior radio operator. He informed me that I was being sent to Battle Group Wegener in Olshana. Olshana had been split off from the main pocket and was soon to be relieved. Despite my ailing foot, I drove the Kfz. 17 myself. I didn't have to drive all the way to Olshana, as the Wegener Group's command post was situated outside the town. After two or three days, the encircled units (including SS Pioneer Battalion 5) fought their way through to us. I then had to go see the doctor, who, after disinfecting the foot, operated on me in an old school with no anesthetic and under increasingly heavy mortar fire. I was supposed to go to the rear echelon to recover, but that evening the order came for everyone to prepare to move out. Excess ballast was to be discarded. All of our signals documents, in particular, had to be destroyed. Departure began the next morning. I was supposed to go to Korsun, to be flown out of the pocket. Five Ju 52s were waiting there. The jostling for places in the aircraft was so terrible that one had to use force to obtain a seat.*

After the third Ju 52 to take off was shot down, I asked my comrades to take me back to the unit. In the evening the order came from our division commander Gille that henceforth movement on the roads must be limited to supply and radio vehicles. He emphasized that materiel no longer mattered, only the people. From Korsun we drove to Stablov. It resembled a flight. Then we moved on to Shanderovka, the heart of the pocket. Our older comrades of the rear-echelon services offered us the last of their tobacco products with the request that we not abandon them now. We were tormented by hunger, having been issued our last rations in Stablov: a can of rice for eight men! It was eaten the way it was, frozen.

Preparations for the breakout were completed on the evening of 16 February 1944. We stood by on the road out of Shanderovka. We were still in radio communications with the "Germania" Regiment and with our reconnaissance battalion. Moving silently, at about 23:00 hours the "Westland" Regiment broke through the first Russian lines. We followed in the radio truck. Suddenly we became stuck. My friend Kokro threw open the door and screamed: 'everyone out, we're lost'. That was at 05:30 in the morning on 17 February 1944. From there we continued on foot, as fast as we could go. Our vehicle was blown up. I walked without crutches—no thought of those any more. What I saw was a hopeless flight. Thousands of men moved across a broad expanse. Shells burst among them. I recalled a picture of Napoleon's retreat from Russia. I believe it had hung in our classroom. After two hours we came to a gully and were finally able to catch our breath. We came to a village that had just been taken by our advance guards of the "Westland" Regiment. A self-propelled 150-mm gun, our people clustered on it, drove forward. The village lay under heavy artillery fire. T 34s attacked. In one house there were Russians wounded. The lady of the house gave everyone tea. The flight continued in heavy snow showers. Another village. We cautiously bypassed it. A forest swallowed us up. Swamp and thickets. The panye wagons on which we were evacuating our wounded could go no farther. The Russian panye drivers fled. The horses broke free. Near Lysyanka the forest became a forest of death. The Lysyanka River lay before us. A vast crowd of men piled up on the east bank. The German main line of resistance was supposed to be on the other side of the river. There was no bridge of any kind. Ice and the bodies of horses floated in the river. A dying man asked me to say hello to his mother. He was unable to tell me her address. Another asked for help. I promised it to him, but there was nothing I could do. I was at least able to grant the request of one comrade, half frozen in the mud, by tossing him a wool blanket. Suddenly we came under anti-tank fire from the forest. Very few still had weapons and only a few had the strength to resist, however after a few bursts of ammunition were fired into the forest the firing died down. Finally we discovered a makeshift footbridge: wagons tied together with rope. It was at least a possibility, but hundreds of men clogged the bridge. Suddenly there was another outburst of tank fire. Everyone scattered and took cover. Only

Elements of the 5th SS Panzer Division "*Wiking*" fought in the Kovel area from the end of March to the beginning of May 1944.

Division commander SS-Gruppenführer Gille with SS-Sturmbannführer Ullrich.

a few stalwarts took the chance and crossed the river, up to their chests in water. On the other side we crawled away on all fours. The frozen bodies of comrades showed us the way. Wearily I dragged myself along. Suddenly my friend Hans Teng shouted: "Schnorsch, German lookouts!" They were men of the Leibstandarte in white snow jackets. It had taken us three hours to cover three kilometers! We found shelter in a packed village schoolhouse. Exhausted, I lay down on the floor. The warmth felt good, but my clothing thawed out and I became soaked to the skin. We had not yet reached freedom, however. Again we set out across the flat steppe, for the spearhead that had reached us was only about 2 km wide. And so on 18 February 1944 we walked another 30 to 40 km in the cold under artillery and small arms fire. Our goal was Risino. There another surprise was waiting for us. The place was in enemy hands. The 19th of February wasn't much easier—20 to 30 km to Buki—but by evening we had made it."

The approximately 4,000 survivors of the 5th SS Panzer Division "*Wiking*" assembled without weapons and vehicles near Risino (approx. 25 km west of Zvenigorodka). At the end of February-beginning of March the division moved through Rumania into the area east of Lublin. Approximately 8,000 men had been killed, wounded or captured by the Soviets. On 16 March 1944 the division command received orders for transport to Kovel, about 140 km to the east. The division was to rest and reequip in the camp there and also provide a reserve for the nearby front.

While *SS-Gruppenführer* Gille flew to Kovel, the trains carrying the division were halted by partisans about 50 kilometers from the city, and the troops were forced to carry out a time-consuming operation to clear the rail line. Before they could reach the city the important transportation center was encircled by Soviet troops. On 17 March 1944 Hitler declared it a "fortified place" under the command of *SS-Gruppenführer* Gille.

By 21 March 1944 a German relief force had assembled in the Maciejów area. In addition to elements of the 131st Infantry Division and Assault Gun Battalion 190, this included the newly-formed III (Armored) Battalion, SS Panzer Grenadier Regiment 9 "*Germania*", just arrived from France, and the II (Panther) Battalion, SS Panzer Regiment 5, also a new unit. Other elements of the 5th SS Panzer Division "*Wiking*" were deployed to guard the flanks.

The relief attempt began on 29 March 1944. The next day elements of II Battalion, SS Panzer Regiment 5 broke through to Kovel to reinforce the encircled forces. When the available forces proved insufficient to crack the Soviet ring around Kovel, LVI Panzer Corps was sent in with the 4th and 5th Panzer Divisions.

On 4 April 1944 elements of the 5th SS Panzer Division, together with the two army panzer divisions, began another relief attempt. In fierce fighting the troops successfully breached the numerous Soviet anti-tank fronts, and the next

The difficult fighting withdrawal in 1944.

day entered the city from the north. From there the units advanced to the west and southwest to establish contact with the 131st Infantry Division. Kovel had been liberated in heavy fighting. Elements of the division remained in the Kovel area until the beginning of May 1944 to further solidify the front. With the exception of the newly-formed units, which remained in the Kovel area attached to LVI Panzer Corps, the division was ordered to Training Camp "Heidelager" for a complete refit.

Following the addition of ethnic Germans from southeastern Europe, plus men returned from leave and convalescents, on 30 June 1944 the division was able to report a strength of:

Officers	NCOs	Enlisted Men	Total
435	3,066	13,847	17,348
2.9%	18.8%	78.3%	100%

In mid-July 1944 the unit was moved into the hotly-contested Bialowieza area (approx. 65 km southeast of Bialystok), approximately 380 kilometers away. Since 16 July 1944 the units still at the front (III Battalion, SS Panzer Grenadier Regiment 9 and II Battalion, SS Panzer Regiment 5) had been battling advancing enemy forces. While still en route to the front, the units were advised of a new area

Map: actions by the 5th SS Panzer Division "*Wiking*" in July – August 1944.

of operations. On 19 July they occupied a bridgehead along the Leśna River near Kamieniec Litewski (approx. 39 km northeast of Brest Litovsk) in the XX Army Corps's sector (2nd Army) to prepare to meet the rapidly approaching Soviet tank units.

The 5th SS Panzer Division "*Wiking*" was, however, unable to even partially stabilize Army Group Center's shattered front. Instead, it became caught up in the chaotic retreat, and in the following two weeks it was forced to withdraw about 160 kilometers to the southwest. After crossing the Bug, at the end of July the unit occupied positions near Stanislawów with front to the south and west. The division was now attached to the newly-created IV SS Panzer Corps (2nd Army). There was no continuous main line of resistance to the 9th Army near Warsaw. On 3 August 1944 an attack was begun towards Okuniew in the west. Contact was supposed to be established with elements of the XXXIX Panzer Corps attacking from the Warsaw area. After successfully closing the gap in the front, the 5th SS Panzer Division's main line of resistance ran from Stanislawów approximately 10 kilometers in a westerly direction. On 10 August 1944 *SS-Gruppenführer* Gille took command of the IV SS Panzer Corps (now 9th Army). *SS-Standartenführer* Mühlenkamp was subsequently placed in command of the 5th SS Panzer Division.

In the course of a shortening of the front, on the night of 12 August 1944 the unit changed positions with the 3rd SS Panzer Division "*Totenkopf*" and moved back to a position just under 20 km to the north. The 5th SS Panzer Division's strength at that time was:

5 average strength panzer grenadier battalions[20]
6 light artillery batteries (30 105-mm field howitzers)
4 heavy artillery batteries (18 150-mm field howitzers)
11 heavy anti-tank guns (75-mm)
12 assault guns
16 Panzer IV
21 Panzer V Panther

On 14 August 1944, following a heavy artillery bombardment, enemy forces broke through the 3rd SS Panzer Division on the right. Counterattacks proved futile. Four days later a hurricane-like barrage of artillery fire opened the Battle of Warsaw. In addition to further fierce fighting at the seam with the 3rd SS Panzer

[20] The panzer grenadiers' combined combat strength was about 2,000 men. SS Panzer Grenadier Regiment "*Narva*", which functioned as III Battalion, SS Panzer Grenadier Regiment 10 "*Westland*", had been discharged from the unit and transferred to the 20th SS Volunteer Grenadier Division (Estonian No. 1). A new III Battalion made up of Ukrainian SS volunteers was under formation. SS Armored Reconnaissance Battalion 5 was in Germany for rest and reorganization.

Panzer V Panthers (Ausf. A) of II Battalion, SS Panzer Regiment 5 "*Wiking*".

Division, there were also critical situations at the boundary with the unit on the left, which was also the boundary with the XX Army Corps (2nd Army).

As the 5th SS Panzer Division lacked the forces to reestablish contact, reinforcements, including Grenadier Brigade 1131, were rushed to SS Panzer Grenadier Regiment "*Westland*" fighting on the left wing. However, the units were incapable of withstanding the massive Soviet attacks by as many as seven divisions. On 24 August 1944 the division, in the line Radzymin – Nieporet (approx. 10 km west of Radzymin), reported a combat strength of 2,065 men out of a rations strength of 10,335 men. The unit had lost almost exactly 7,000 men killed, wounded, or missing in just under two months.

By 6 September 1944 the unit was forced to pull back across the Narev and occupied a 12-kilometers-long main line of resistance from Serock to south of Nieporet in the so-called "wet triangle"[21]. The unit, now assessed as "*only conditionally capable of defense*", still had nine batteries of artillery with a total of 35 howitzers.

In order to raise its fighting strength, the 5th SS Panzer Division was sent III Battalion, SS Panzer Grenadier Regiment 10 "*Westland*", made up largely of Ukrainians, and about 1,000 members of the Luftwaffe who had been transferred to the *Waffen-SS* but lacked infantry experience. On 25 September 1944 the fierce and very costly fighting died down. On 2 October 1944 the 5th SS Panzer Division reported the following strengths:

I/SS Panzer Grenadier Regiment 9	193 men
II/SS Panzer Grenadier Regiment 9	396 men
III/SS Panzer Grenadier Regiment 9	176 men
I/SS Panzer Grenadier Regiment 10	527 men
II/SS Panzer Grenadier Regiment 10	332 men
III/SS Panzer Grenadier Regiment 10	548 men
SS Armored Pioneer Battalion 5	384 men
SS Armored Reconnaissance Battalion 5	325 men

The division's total combat strength was thus approximately 5,000 men and its rations strength about 10,000 men. On 10 October 1944 the Red Army renewed its offensive. Fierce fighting raged until 28 October, and there were penetrations of the German main line of resistance. Costly counterattacks prevented the front from collapsing, although the defenders were forced to fall back to a position approximately 12 km farther to the west (under the command of *SS-Standartenführer* Ullrich).

21 The name "Wet Triangle" refers to the very marshy region between the Bug and the Vistula. The triangle was closed in the east by the main line of resistance.

Actions by the 5th SS Panzer Division "*Wiking*" (January – May 1945).

BMW R-75 of SS Panzer Regiment 5 "*Wiking*".

The offensive in Hungary literally became "stuck in the mud". Animals and machines frequently reached the point of total exhaustion.

Medium armored troop carrier (Sd.Kfz. 251 Ausf. C).

While every enemy attack and artillery bombardment, plus the categorically initiated counterattacks decimated the German units and supply, thanks to their superiority in numbers the Soviets were able to gain ground steadily.

On 16 November 1944 the surviving Ukrainian volunteers of III Battalion, SS Panzer Grenadier Regiment 10 were released to return to the 14th Waffen Grenadier Division (Galician No. 1). The newly formed first battalions of the SS Panzer Grenadier Regiments 23 "*Norge*" and 24 "*Danmark*" were sent to the 5th SS Panzer Division to take their place.[22] Additional members of the Luftwaffe were also transferred to the division.

When the Hungarian capital was encircled by the Red Army at Christmas 1944, the IV SS Panzer Corps received orders to move to Army Group South. While the corps headquarters and the 3rd SS Panzer Division were withdrawn from action near Modlin on 25 December, the 5th SS Panzer Division briefly came under the command of XXXVI Panzer Corps. Soon afterwards the units began entraining for transport to Army Group Balck in Raab. From there they marched approximately 50 kilometers east to the jumping off positions in front of Tata. By the time the attack order for the relief of Budapest, roughly 60 kilometers away, was issued on 1 January 1945, only 28 of the total of 87 trains transporting the 5th SS Panzer Division had arrived.

Advancing across hilly, wooded terrain, the attackers were able to take Tata. Because of the difficult terrain, SS Armored Artillery Regiment 5 was only able to provide limited support. SS Panzer Grenadier Regiment 9 "*Germania*" and I Battalion, SS Panzer Grenadier Regiment 23 "*Norge*" occupied Torjan on 3 January 1945, receiving a tumultuous welcome from the Hungarian population. After the rest of the division arrived in Hungary, the two panzer grenadier regiments launched a combined attack, and on 5 January reached Bicske. An attempt to take Martonvasar failed and the attack was halted. "Operation Konrad", the first attempt to relieve Budapest, had failed.

Army Group South redeployed its forces and began planning "Operation Konrad 2". SS Panzer Grenadier Regiment 10 "*Westland*" was ordered into the area south of Gran. The second relief plan called for the regiment to attack through the Pilis Mountains. After Piliszentkereszt was taken, the commanding general of the IV SS Panzer Corps, *SS-Obergruppenführer* Gille, ordered SS Panzer Grenadier Regiment 9 "*Germania*" into the attack area to exploit the success.

When the committed elements of the 5th SS Panzer Division were about 17 kilometers from Budapest, Hitler, misreading the situation, ordered the attack halted. The next day I Battalion, SS Panzer Grenadier Regiment 24 "*Danmark*" was attached to the 6th Panzer Division, while I Battalion, SS Panzer Grenadier Regiment 23 "*Norge*" and I Battalion, SS Panzer Grenadier Regiment 9 "*Germania*"

[22] These actually belonged to the 11th SS Volunteer Panzer Grenadier Division "*Nordland*".

were attached to the 3rd Cavalry Brigade.[23] Within the IV SS Panzer Corps, the 5th SS Panzer Division moved about 80 kilometers to the south into the Csajag area on Lake Balaton.

From there, on 18 January 1945 the units were supposed to take part in the so-called southern solution for the relief of Budapest ("Operation Konrad 3"). After heavy fighting the units were able to break into the Soviet main line of resistance near Balatonfö-Kajar. The next day the troops crossed the Sárviz Canal east of Kàloz, 20 km away, and then turned north toward Sarosd, approximately 16 km distant. From there the 5th SS Panzer Division drove northeast, and on 23 January reached the Danube near Adony. Budapest was still 45 kilometers away. Finally the division reached the Vali River. Faced with an in-depth Soviet defense and hampered by frequent changes of orders from Army Group Balck, the advance came to a halt. The units were forced to go over to the defensive between Baracska and Adony.

On 29 January 1945 the Soviets launched their own offensive, and the next day they achieved deep penetrations into the 5th SS Panzer Division's main line of resistance. Now attached to III Panzer Corps, the division began withdrawing to the line Gárdony – Szolgaeghyáza. With no continuous German front, the enemy was also able to advance to the west near Seregelyes. On 4-5 February 1945, therefore, the unit moved into the Margarethe Position in front of Stuhlweissenburg (Hungarian = Székesfehérvár).

Because of its numerical weakness, on 6 February 1945 the 5th SS Panzer Division was designated a battle group, and four days later it came under the command of IV SS Panzer Corps. On 22 February 1945, after about two weeks of quiet at the front, it was moved into the area on either side of Stuhlweissenburg. The battle group received replacements, mainly from the air force and navy, and on 27 February 1945 it was designated the 5th SS Panzer Division again.

The quiet at the front ended on 16 March 1945. After a heavy barrage, the Red Army attacked in the Stuhlweissenburg area. While the neighboring 3rd SS Panzer Division was forced to the west, the 5th SS Panzer Division was initially able to hold its positions. On 10 March 1945 it possessed the following equipment (less than 50% of which was mobile):

4 Panzer IV
13 Panzer V Panther
8 assault guns
6 batteries of light artillery
4 batteries of heavy artillery

[23] The two regiments took part in the fighting for Stuhlweissenburg with the 1st Panzer Division, separate from the 5th SS Panzer Division "*Wiking*", and on 23 January 1945 were tactically attached to the 3rd SS Panzer Division "*Totenkopf*".

The panzer regiment's strength was thus equivalent to three weak companies and it had no fuel. On 21 March 1945, with the encirclement of the city imminent, *SS-Oberführer* Ullrich decided—contrary to Hitler's orders—to pull out his units. Moving northwest past Lake Balaton, the division lost almost all of its armored vehicles and heavy weapons due to lack of fuel.

With no firm main line of resistance and disintegration setting in, the exhausted units tried to reach the west. On 24 March 1945 a halt line was set up temporarily around Veszprém. Behind the line the units that had been so badly battered in recent days were to be issued replacements. The commander of SS Armored Signals Battalion 5, *SS-Sturmbannführer* Schmeißer, remembered:

"The new replacements came from home-based units that had been raised in the cities for the Security and Aid Service (SHD), to be used to help out in air raids and fight fires; there were young anti-aircraft auxiliaries too. Our replacements were either children or old men between 50 and 60. In SS Armored Signals Battalion 5 they were placed in the train, because they lacked any kind of combat experience. The men whose places they took were assigned to battle groups."

It was not just the rapid advance by the Red Army, which by 29 March 1945 had forced the remnants of the 5th SS Panzer Division back toward the Raab bridgehead at Vasvar (Eisenburg) after fighting at Sümeg, that prevented a restoration of operational capability. The soldiers had covered approximately 130 kilometers in about a week. Orders were issued to occupy the Reich Defense Position in the area southeast of Fürstenfeld, approximately 60 away. After further heavy fighting, on 7 May 1945 the first units withdrew from that area of operations in order to proceed to the demarcation line on the Enns, roughly 160 kilometers away.

The units moved via Graz and Radstadt to the Klein Arl Valley, where they were taken prisoner by the Americans. Thus, the operational career of the 5th SS Panzer Division ended after just under four years of existence. The unit had taken part in the rapid and frequently unopposed advance into the Caucasus, as well as the fierce and extremely costly fighting withdrawal that began at the end of 1942. In March 1945 operations almost led to the disbandment of the division. It is interesting to note that propaganda claims that the unit consisted of "Germanic" volunteers was untrue. By 1945 not even 5% of the division's members were northern- or western-European volunteers. By that time there were only about 350 Flemish volunteers left in the division's ranks.

The 27th SS Volunteer Grenadier Division "*Langemarck*" (Flemish No. 1)

The Volunteer Legion "*Flandern*"[24]

As previously mentioned, the number of Flemish men who volunteered for the *Waffen-SS* remained far below expectations. This was in part due to the disinterest in Himmler's plans and objectives on the part of the largest Flemish collaborationist organization (VNV), and also to the strict entrance requirements (for the volunteers of the DeVlag).

The authorities were loath to lose the volunteers who were unable to meet the *Waffen-SS* entrance requirements, however, and on 10 April 1941 formation of the SS Volunteer Unit "*Nordwest*" began in Hamburg-Langenhorn. The entrance requirements were eased to allow for the creation of two *Standarten* (regiments)[25] made up of Flemish and Dutch personnel.

The first men left Belgium on 14 April 1941. Two more transports followed on the 28th of April and the 21st of May. The Flemish volunteers were sworn in on 21 June 1941, and at the end of July 1941 the unit was transferred to Training Camp Debica[26]. With the recruitment effort still failing to achieve the desired results, on 6 August the volunteer unit was renamed SS Volunteer Standarte "*Nordwest*". Flemish troops formed the:

1st Company, SS Volunteer Standarte "*Nordwest*"
6th Company, SS Volunteer Standarte "*Nordwest*"
8th Company, SS Volunteer Standarte "*Nordwest*"

At Debica, the companies were bolstered by 405 volunteers who had left Brussels on 6 August 1941. In September the *Standarte* moved to Training Camp Arys in East Prussia. At that time the Flemish *Sturmbann* (battalion) of the *Standarte "Nordwest"* reported a strength of:

[24] In Flemish/Dutch the title is *Vrijwilligers-Legioen Vlaanderen*.

[25] While applicants for the SS Standarte "*Westland*" had to be between the ages of 17 and 25 years and be at least 1.74 meters tall, volunteers for the SS Standarte "*Nordwest*" and later the Legion "*Flandern*" could be up to 40 years of age, while the height requirement was 1.65 meters.

[26] The training camp was renamed SS Training Camp "Heidelager" on 15 March 1943.

Vrijwilligers-Legioen Vlaanderen

den 194

GESTELLUNGSBEFEHL

für die „Vrijwilligers-Legioen Vlaanderen"

Auf Grund Ihrer Verpflichtung werden Sie hierdurch einberufen und haben sich
am ....194..... bis.......................Uhr
in ....
unter Vorlage dieses Gestellungsbefehls zu melden.
Es ist mitzubringen:

1. Mundvorrat für 2 Tage.
2. Toiletteartikel (Rasierzeug, Zahnbürste, Kamm, Schuhputzzeug).
3. Koffer oder Schachtel zur Zurücksendung der Zivilkleidung.
4. Urkunden über abgeleistete Dienstzeit und erreichten Dienstgrad im belg-Heer.

Ersatzkommando Flandern u. Wallonien
der Waffen-SS

für ....

von Bahnhof ....
nach Bahnhof ....
Dienstgrad und Name des Reisenden: ....
(bei mehreren des Transportführers)

Zweck und Veranlassung der Reise: **Einberufung zur « Vrijwilligers-Legioen Vlaanderen ».**
Eigenmächtiges Benutzen einer höheren Wagenklasse ist verboten. Dieser Ausweis ist **nur** den Kontrollorganen der Wehrmacht vorzuzeigen und am Zielbahnhof an diese abzugeben. Sind solche nicht vorhanden, so ist er nach Beendigung der Reise an die Wehrmachtdienststelle abzugeben.

Ausgefertigt am..194....

Ersatzkommando Flandern u. Wallonien
der Waffen-SS

Dienststempel

(Unterschrift)

Induction order form for the Volunteer Legion "*Flanders*". The photo shows volunteers of the Zwarte Brigade for the Legion "*Flanders*".

Officers	NCOs	Enlisted Men	Total
25	78	1,009	1,112
2.25%	7%	90.75%	100%

In addition to 162 German core personnel, the units included 950 Flemings:

Officers	NCOs	Enlisted Men	Total
14	1	935	950
1.26%	.09%	84.08%	85.43%

The fact that just 15 of the unit's more than 100 officers and non-commissioned officers were Flemish soon caused the volunteers' motivation to sink. One thinks of the letter written by the leader of the VNV Staf de Clerq in March 1942 concerning the treatment of the Flemish soldiers by the German core personnel.[27]

The late arrivals were sworn in at Training Camp Arys in October 1941. The SS Volunteer *Standarte "Nordwest"* was disbanded on 6 November 1941. For political reasons the men were used to form two volunteer legions, "*Flandern*" and "*Niederlände*". This was done in response to the desire on the part of the foreigners to serve in their own units in the war against communism. One former member remembered:

"The Vlaams Legioen was created soon after the war against the Soviet Union broke out. In Flanders it was believed that the legion would be a sort of Free Corps which, though part of the Waffen-SS, would be very closely modeled on the VNV. The Vlaams Nationaal Verbond had been a political party before the war, and after 28 May 1940 it had continued to follow its Flemish-nationalist agenda with the blessing of the Germans. The VNV was pro-German, because it realized that its fate was tied to that of Germany. After the war against the Soviet Union began, the leader of the VNV was determined that a Flemish legion should take part in the fight on the Eastern Front. Out of a desire to demonstrate independence, the unit's troops wore a three-armed sun wheel on their collar tabs instead of the SS runes. The majority of the volunteers who joined the legion came from the ranks of the VNV or the NSJV youth movement."

[27] See the chapter: "Belgians in German Military Service"

Members of the Volunteer Legion "*Flanders*" at the Volkhov River front.

For Germany, the main value of the independent legions was a propaganda one. Formation of the foreign legions was touted as participation by Western European nations in the "ideological war". On 6 November 1941 Himmler declared:

"The Führer has approved the participation of foreign volunteers in the war against Bolshevism. This participation will, however, take place in closed formations under their own command. Given adequate recruitment, foreign volunteers of related blood – Danes, Flemings, Netherlanders and Norwegians – will be formed into volunteer Legions by the SS-FHA and incorporated into the Waffen-SS."

This incorporation did not mean direct membership, however, and the unit designations consciously avoided use of the "SS" prefix. The foreign soldiers were given SS pay books and ranks; however, the rank designations were altered, with the word "*Legions-*" replacing the "SS", for example, *Legions-Untersturmführer* instead of *SS-Untersturmführer*.

By November 1941 the men of the former SS Volunteer *Standarte "Nordwest"* had completed six months of training. On 6 November Himmler placed them under the command of the 2nd SS Motorized Infantry Brigade, which was stationed in the army's rear area. On 10 November the legion arrived in the Tosno – Adrianova area by way of Mitau – Tauroggen – Riga – Valga – Dorpat. Together with two Latvian police battalions[28], which arrived at about the same time, it relieved the 4th SS Motorized Infantry Regiment. Initially employed in the anti-partisan role, on 3 December 1941 the legion was moved to the front. For a week the Flemish troops under Legion commander *SS-Obersturmbannführer* Lippert were deployed in the Maluska area (between Mag and Kirischi). They were then moved via Tosno – Lugo – Pskov – Riga to winter quarters in Kandau (Latvian Kandava) in the Kurische Schweiz (a valley between Kandava and Sabile in present-day Latvia).

After about four weeks of quiet, on 10 January 1942 the unit was dispatched to the Novgorod area in anticipation of a major Soviet offensive along the Volkhov River. There the legion was combined with the Escort Battalion "*Reichsführer-SS*" and the SS Flak Battalion to form Battle Group "Debes"[29]. From 19 January 1942 the legion saw action in the Podberesye area (approx. 20 km northwest of Novgorod) as part of XXXVIII Army Corps. Enduring temperatures as low as minus 50 degrees, the troops attempted to sever the Soviet 2nd Shock Army's rearward communications west of the Volkhov. Fierce offensive and defensive fighting

[28] See Michaelis, Rolf: *Letten in der Ordnungspolizei und Waffen-SS*, Berlin 2009.

[29] After *SS-Oberführer* Debes was given command of SS Infantry Regiment 9, *SS-Sturmbannführer* Burk assumed command of the regiment-strength SS Battle Group "Debes".

Approximately 800 Flemings were killed while serving in the *Waffen-SS* on the Eastern Front.

The grave of Karsten Johannson, killed on 27/1/1942 while serving in the Volunteer Legion "*Flanders*" in the Podberezhye area.

resulted in the Flemish troops receiving mention in the Wehrmacht communiqué of 10 February 1942:

"*The 25th Motorized Infantry Division from Württemberg and the SS Legion 'Flanders' distinguished themselves in the successful defense against the heaviest mass attacks by the enemy.*"

The Flemish troops again received mention on 4 March 1942:

"*Enemy attacks at various places in the central and northern sectors of the front were unsuccessful. Several localized counterattacks drove the enemy from his positions. The SS Legion 'Flanders' took 25 enemy bunkers in bitter close-quarters fighting.*"

On 24 March the Volunteer Legion "*Flandern*" reported its losses to date on the Russian Front:

	Officers	Other Ranks
Killed	4	74
Wounded	11	428

The Legion's casualties, especially in the fighting after 19 January 1942, were thus equal to about 50% of its original strength. After several days of rest, the Flemish volunteers returned to the back-and-forth struggle to complete the closure and reduction of the Volkhov pocket. On 2 April 1942 the Legion's commander was seriously wounded and replaced by *SS-Sturmbannführer* Fitzthum. At the end of April 1942 the Soviets launched an offensive by the 59th Army in an attempt to restore contact with its encircled troops. When this failed, the Commander-in-Chief of the Volkhov Front ordered the evacuation of the 2nd Shock Army.

To prevent this, the German 18th Army ordered an offensive to begin on 22 May 1942. Nine days later the pocket was closed for good. During this period the Volunteer Legion "*Flandern*" was attached to Battle Group "*Hoppe*", which was organized as follows:

Security Battalion 232
III Battalion, Infantry Regiment 262 [250th Infantry Division (Spanish)]
Reconnaissance Battalion 250 [250th Infantry Division (Spanish)]
SS Battle Group "Burk" with
  Volunteer Legion "*Flandern*"
  Escort Battalion "*Reichsführer-SS*"
  SS Flak Battalion "East"

III Battalion, Artillery Regiment 126
a mixed battalion from the 20th Infantry Division

The battle group was supposed to advance north through the pocket and link up with German troops coming the other way from Krechno. By the end of June 1942, after this successful but costly operation, the encircled Soviet 2nd Shock Army was completely destroyed. At the end of June 1942 the Flemings were pulled out of the front and transferred to the Osiya rest area (southeast of Selo Gora) near the front. There *SS-Hauptsturmführer* Schellong assumed command of the Volunteer Legion, whose seriously depleted ranks were filled with new replacements.

Four weeks later the Legion was moved to the Leningrad Front as part of the 2nd SS Motorized Infantry Brigade. Attached to I Army Corps, the unit marched into the area south of Pulkovo (17 km south of Leningrad) to west of Pushkin. On its left was the Latvian Legion and on its right the 250th Infantry Division (Spanish). Manning a four-kilometer-long section of front that stuck into the Soviet main line of resistance like a thorn, the Flemish troops held their exposed position for almost six months despite fierce enemy attacks. On 31 December 1942 the Legion command submitted the following strength report:

Officers	Other Ranks	Total
21	664	685
3.1%	96.9%	100%
Flemish numbers		
2	626	628

Of the 950 Flemings in November 1941, only about 628 were now left. To date, more than 300 had been killed or seriously wounded. The officer corps was still almost exclusively German. There were only two Flemish officers in the ranks of the Legion.

The members of the Volunteer Legion "*Flanders*" and the SS Assault Brigade "*Langemarck*" wore a national shield bearing the Flemish Lion, while the former also wore cuff titles.

At the end of January 1943, the Volunteer Legion "*Flandern*" was relieved by elements of the SS Police Division and transferred into the area west of Krasny Bor. There it rested for about three weeks as corps reserve. During the course of the Soviet winter offensive the Flemings were attached to the hard-pressed SS Police Division. From 25 February 1943 there was fierce fighting in the bend of the Neva River north of Krasny Bor, during which the Red Army made repeated attempts to cross the frozen river. In mid-March 1943 the Legion was made corps reserve again and was moved to Szablino (approx. 10 km south of Krasny Bor). On 22 March fierce fighting again broke out, with the Legion defending the Krasny Bor area. Within a week the Legion was all but destroyed. All that was left of its original strength of 500 men was a platoon of 50 soldiers! All of the others had been killed or wounded. On 1 April 1943, what was left of the Legion was assembled in Szablino, where it received 250 replacements (some of whom were convalescents). On 13 May 1943 the Volunteer Legion "*Flandern*" was sent to SS Training Camp Heidelager for expansion into the SS Volunteer Assault Brigade "*Langemarck*".

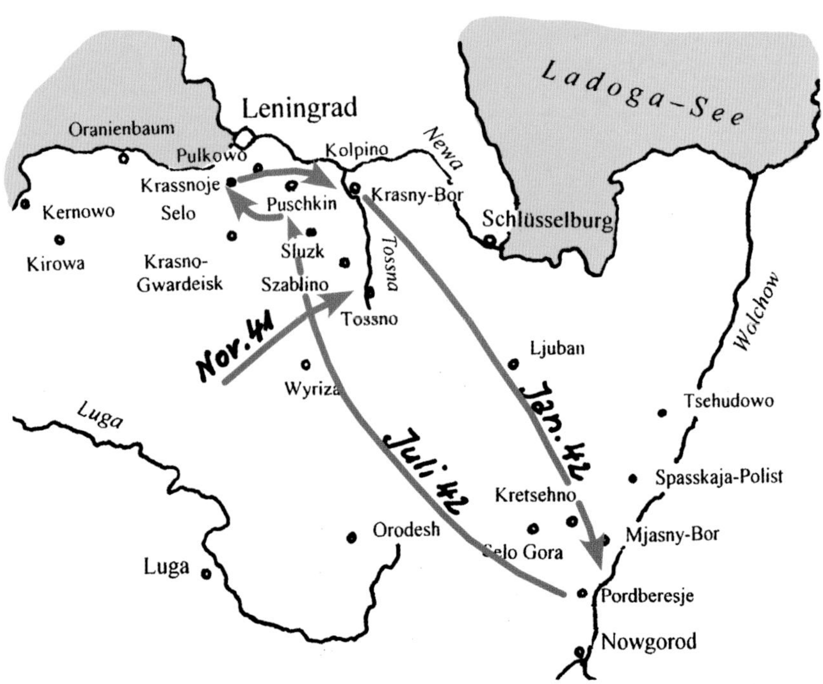

Map: Areas of operations of the Volunteer Legion "*Flanders*" (November 1941 – May 1943).

A former member recalled:

*"I was born in Flanders on 15 January 1925 and as a seventeen-year-old volunteered for the 'Vlaams Legioen'. On 23 July 1942 I went to the town hall in Kortrijk where physical examinations were being conducted on Flemish volunteers for the Volunteer Legion 'Flandern'. Volunteers for the Waffen-SS (*SS-Regiment *'Westland') were also taking physicals. All of our information was taken down: height, weight, chest measurement, vision, etc. I noted with concern that most of those ahead of me were not being assessed particularly well. They were all taller fellows than I at 165 cm. I was therefore all the more surprised when an SS officer asked me if I would like to volunteer directly for the Waffen-SS, even though its minimum height requirement was 168 cm. I, however, stuck to my intention of joining the 'Vlaams Legioen'. I was called up on 10 August 1942 and ordered to present myself in Antwerp. We received our initial training in black Belgian uniforms, and several of us were sent home again. In September 1942 we were transferred to the SS training camp in Sennheim, Alsace. There we were issued Waffen-SS field gray uniforms with SS collar patches. Sennheim provided replacements for all the Flemish volunteer units on the Eastern Front, including the Waffen-SS (in particular the* SS-Regiment *'Westland'). In October 1942 the SS volunteers were transferred to Klagenfurt and we to the legions' replacement battalion in Graz. After basic infantry training I was sent to Nuremberg for signals training. In May 1943 I was back in Graz. One day we, the Flemish members of the battalion, were ordered to fall in on the drill square wearing belts and steel helmets. The commanding officer came, and after the usual greeting and salute he read to us an order from the Führer which went something like: the Führer appreciates very much the actions and dedication of the Flemings in the struggle against our common foe. Now a new, powerful unit is being created which will bear the honorable title 'Langemarck'. SS-Sturmbannführer Schellong was to remain as commanding officer. The Flemish Legion was no more. The title 'Flanders' disappeared and instead we were given the name of a small Flemish city—we didn't understand why. Some thought it was because many Germans had fallen there in the First World War, evidenced by a large and beautiful cemetery. Most of us were very downcast: we had volunteered to serve in the Flanders Legion, which embodied a body of thought we valued, not the Waffen-SS! We still wore the three-armed sun wheel on our collar patches, but now they were to be replaced by SS runes. Some comrades spoke out openly against this new situation. A friend of mine, Cyriel Peleman, even refused to wear the SS patches. The majority, however, accepted the new situation—including me. In practical terms there was little else we could do, however it left behind a bad taste!"*

Cuff band of the 6th SS Volunteer Assault Brigade "*Langemarck*".

Conrad Schellong was born in Dresden on 7/2/1910. He assumed command of the Volunteer Legion "*Flanders*" on 10/7/1942 with the rank of SS-Hauptsturmführer. After he was promoted to SS-Sturmbannführer, in the spring of 1943 he took command of the SS Volunteer Assault Brigade "*Langemarck*". He was subsequently promoted to *SS-Obersturmbannführer* and awarded the German Cross in Gold and the Knight's Cross and later commanded SS Volunteer Grenadier Regiment 66 (Flemish No. 1).

The 6th SS Volunteer Assault Brigade "*Langemarck*"

As part of the effort to make good the losses suffered in Stalingrad and Tunisia, a fresh recruiting effort was begun in Belgium and among Flemish armaments workers in Germany with the objective of enlarging the existing volunteer units. Recognizing that, since 1940, recruitment had failed to attract the desired number of volunteers, thought was given to simply drafting the Flemings. As he had done in the Baltic States, Himmler planned to draft entire age classes into the labor service. Those drafted would then have the choice of working in the armaments industry or joining the *Waffen-SS*/police. It was ultimately decided not to take these steps, which were contrary to international law, as it was anticipated that they would lead to unrest and strikes.

During the course of the various reorganizations and raising of new units for the *Waffen-SS*, the Volunteer Legion "*Flandern*" was finally disbanded effective 31 May 1943. Some of the approximately 700 legion members who eventually assembled at SS Training Camp Heidelager were initially sent to the replacement unit, SS Grenadier Training Battalion East in Zhitomir. From there they took part in the anti-partisan operations dubbed Vistula I and II. During these actions, which took place in the so-called "wet triangle", an area of forest and swamps bordered by the Pripyat Marshes in the southwest, the Dniepr in the east, and the Mozyr – Gomel rail line in the north, the Flemish troops took part in the requisitioning of agricultural goods. In mid-June they were transferred into the Ovruch – Mozyr – Leltshitsy – Olovsk – Belekurichi – Ovruch area, where it was believed there were about 20,000 Soviet partisans. Together with the Royal Hungarian VII Army Corps, SS Grenadier Replacement Battalion East was positioned close to Ovruch to prevent the partisans from escaping to the south and east. On 8 July 1943 the Flemings were returned to SS Training Camp Heidelager.

The units were moved to SS Training Camp Böhmen (Bohemia)[30] for the ultimate establishment of the SS Volunteer Assault Brigade "*Langemarck*". With recruitment lagging far behind what was hoped for, as previously mentioned, the physical criteria were further eased, including increasing the age of entrance to 45. As a result of this, at the end of July about 300 new recruits from Ghent arrived in Milowitz. In August 1943 another 400 Flemings arrived in Milowitz, near Prague,[31] from the legions' former replacement battalion in Graz by way of the SS Grenadier Training Battalion East in Breslau.

---

[30] In September 1943, SS Training Camp "Milowitz" was renamed SS Training Camp "Böhmen".

[31] The replacement training unit had been the Legion Replacement Battalion in Graz. This was now renamed SS Panzer Grenadier Training and Replacement Battalion 11 and was the replacement training unit for the 11th SS Volunteer Panzer Grenadier Division "*Nordland*". The SS Grenadier Replacement Battalion "Ost" was initially the replacement training unit for the new SS Volunteer Assault Brigade "*Langemarck*", while the specialists retained their respective replacement training units. It was renamed SS Grenadier Replacement Battalion 31 on 1 November 1943.

Jaan Hendrickx was initially taken into the Replacement Battalion of the SS-Regiment "*Westland*" and in 1943 was transferred to the SS Volunteer Assault Brigade "Langemarck".

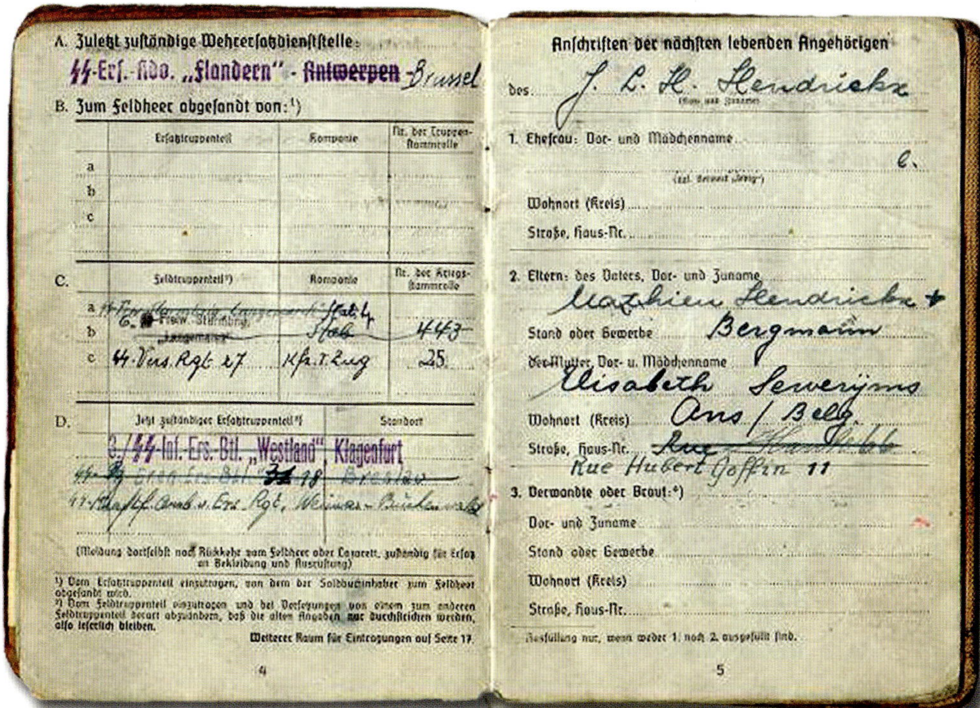

A. Zuletzt zuständige Wehrersatzdienststelle:
SS-Ers.-Kdo. „Flandern" - ~~Antwerpen~~ Brussel
B. Zum Feldheer abgesandt von:¹)

	Ersatztruppenteil	Kompanie	Nr. der Truppen-Stammrolle
a			
b			
c			

C.	Feldtruppenteil²)	Kompanie	Nr. der Kriegs-Stammrolle
a	~~[illegible]~~	~~Stab~~	
b	6. SS-Freiw. Sturmbrig. ~~Langemarck~~	~~Stab~~	443
c	SS-Div. Rgt. 27	Kfz.T.Zug	25

D.	Jetzt zuständiger Ersatztruppenteil²)	Standort
	3./SS-Inf.-Ers.-Btl. „Westland"	Klagenfurt
	~~SS-Pz. Gren. Ers. Btl. 18~~	~~Breslau~~
	SS-Panz.Gren.Ausb.u.Ers.Rgt.	Weimar-Buchenwald

(Meldung dortselbst nach Rückkehr vom Feldheer oder Lazarett, zuständig für Ersatz an Bekleidung und Ausrüstung)

¹) Vom Ersatztruppenteil einzutragen, von dem der Soldbuchinhaber zum Feldheer abgesandt wird.
²) Vom Feldtruppenteil einzutragen und bei Versetzungen von einem zum anderen Feldtruppenteil derart abzuändern, daß die alten Angaben nur durchstrichen werden, also leserlich bleiben.

Weiterer Raum für Eintragungen auf Seite 17.

4

Anschriften der nächsten lebenden Angehörigen
des J. L. H. Hendrickx
(Vor- und Zuname)
1. Ehefrau: Vor- und Mädchenname
(ggf. Vermerk „ledig")
Wohnort (Kreis)
Straße, Haus-Nr.
2. Eltern: des Vaters, Vor- und Zuname
Mathieu Hendrickx +
Stand oder Gewerbe Bergmann
der Mutter, Vor- u. Mädchenname
Elisabeth Severijns
Wohnort (Kreis) Ans / Belg.
Straße, Haus-Nr. ~~Rue [illegible]~~
Rue Hubert Goffin 11
3. Verwandte oder Braut:³)
Vor- und Zuname
Stand oder Gewerbe
Wohnort (Kreis)
Straße, Haus-Nr.
³) Ausfüllung nur, wenn weder 1. noch 2. ausgefüllt sind.

5

Hendrickx was born in Wallonia and had a Wallonian father and Flemish mother.

The SS Volunteer Assault Brigade "*Langemarck*" on its way to the Eastern Front.

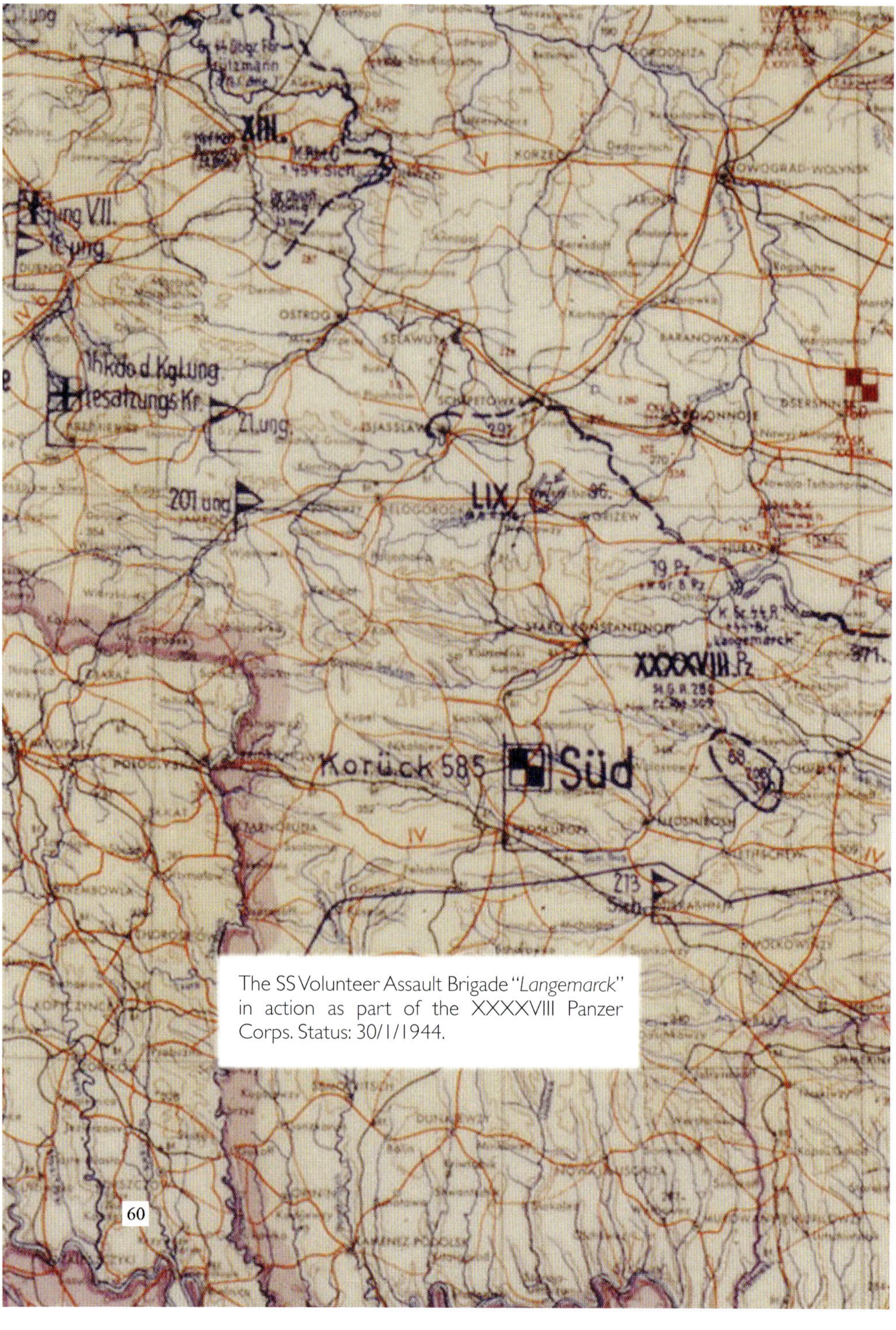

The SS Volunteer Assault Brigade "*Langemarck*" in action as part of the XXXXVIII Panzer Corps. Status: 30/1/1944.

The unit was to be organized as a *Sturmbrigade n.A.* (new type assault brigade):

Brigade Headquarters	SS-Sturmbannführer Schellong
1st Company	SS-Obersturmführer Mahrenholz
2nd Company	SS-Untersturmführer Martenson
3rd Company	SS-Untersturmführer Vogel
4th (Heavy) Company	SS-Untersturmführer Van der Weeën
5th (Infantry Gun) Company	SS-Untersturmführer Köhn
6th (Anti-Tank) Company	SS-Hauptsturmführer Knorr
7th (Assault Gun) Company	SS-Hauptsturmführer Weingärtner
8th (20-mm Flak) Company	SS-Untersturmführer Uyttersprot
9th (88-mm Flak) Company	SS-Untersturmführer Dethier
10th (Supply) Company	SS-Untersturmführer Schaumann

Effective 22 October 1943, during the numbering of *Waffen-SS* units, the brigade was renamed 6th SS Volunteer Assault Brigade "*Langemarck*".[32]

After about six months of training, formation of the unit was considered complete at the beginning of December 1943 and was concluded with a parade in Prague. The unit's strength was equivalent to that of a regiment:

Officers	NCOs	Enlisted Men	Total
40	202	1,774	2,016
2%	10%	88%	100%

With an authorized strength of about 1,700 men, the brigade nominally had about 300 excess members. There were, however, sharp discrepancies at the command level. The unit was short about 20 officers and 300 NCOs, while the unit was over authorized strength in enlisted men by approximately 450. The brigade was therefore not fully prepared for the major battles that lay ahead of it.

At the end of 1943 the Red Army broke through the 4th Panzer Army's main line of resistance (northern wing of Army Group South) along the Kiev to Zhitomir road on a width of about 30 km. Army Group South subsequently moved the 1st

[32] It is interesting that the Flemish unit was given a name that, while that of a town in Flanders, held no historical significance for them. Instead it is the place where, on 10 November 1914, the German XXIII Reserve Corps (mostly green volunteers and reservists) suffered extremely heavy losses when it attacked Belgian-French troops in the First Battle of Flanders. An attempt was later made to create a German heroic epic about the event. The title was appropriate in one respect, however, for the Volunteer Legion "*Flandern*" also suffered very heavy casualties in combat. They were significantly higher than those suffered by the SS volunteers in the SS-Division "*Wiking*" during the same period.

Panzer Army into the threatened area, where, together with the 4th Panzer Army, it was to launch a flanking attack and encircle the Soviet spearheads. Additional units were brought in to bolster the strength of these formations, and on 26 December 1943 6th SS Volunteer Assault Brigade "*Langemarck*" received movement orders to join the 4th Panzer Army. Transported by rail, four days later the Flemish troops reached the main line of resistance near Chudovo (southwest of Zhitomir). The units went straight from the trains into action, helping free a cut-off battle group of the 2nd SS Panzer Grenadier Division "*Das Reich*" of XXXXVIII Panzer Corps. During this action the Langemarck Brigade's 6th (Anti-Tank) Company mistakenly destroyed two of the SS battle group's armored troop carriers!

The unit was employed in an offensive role in the Zhitomir area until 5 January 1944, when Soviet pressure became so great that the units—attached to Battle Group/2nd SS Panzer Grenadier Division "*Das Reich*"—were forced to withdraw toward Severinovka until 11 January. After the enemy shifted the focal point of his attack, the town—now in the 1st Panzer Army's sector—was held until mid-February. On 17 February 1944 the assault brigade was ordered to the left wing of the 1st Panzer Army in the Shepetovka area, about 70 kilometers to the northwest.

The first engagements with advancing enemy forces took place five days later, but just a few days after that orders were received to move to Yampol, situated approximately 60 km to the southwest on the Goryn River. There, on 28 February 1944, the decimated brigade received replacements from Breslau. Positioned at the edge of the Galicia District (in the *Generalgouvernement*), the unit represented the left wing of the 1st Panzer Army. It was a particularly exposed position, for if the enemy broke through there he could roll up the entire front. After enduring extremely heavy fire, on 3 March 1944 a withdrawal was ordered by *SS-Sturmbannführer*

Map: Actions by the 6th SS Volunteer Assault Brigade "Langemarck" in the Ukraine.

Schellong, who was wounded soon afterward. To the west, Soviet forces broke through to the south and then turned east, and the units were encircled. Repeatedly breaking through enemy forces, on 19 March 1944 troops equal to approximately 50% of the unit's original strength reached Starokonstantinov. The town was the scene of heavy close quarters fighting on several days.

Attached to the LIX Panzer Corps, the remnants of the brigade, now under the command of *SS-Hauptsturmführer* Dithier, received orders to occupy positions in Proskurov, approximately 40 kilometers to the south. It was planned that the 1st Panzer Army, which was for all intents encircled with the Dniester at its back, would cross the Zbrucz and break through the Soviet lines to the west. There it would make contact with the 4th Panzer Army. In preparation for the breakout, the remains of the 6th SS Volunteer Assault Brigade "*Langemarck*" and the SS Battle Group "*Das Reich*" were attached to "Corps Group Breith". On 28 March 1944 Corps Group Breith launched its attack toward enemy-held Kamenets-Podolsk, but subsequently bypassed the town. The men reached the Chotin bridgehead position on the Dniepr, all the while in contact with the enemy. While to the north elements of the 1st Panzer Army were able to make contact with units of the 4th Panzer Army advancing to meet them, in the first week of April 1944 the Flemings crossed the Dniester under heavy fire, some swimming. The last of the brigade's vehicles and heavy weapons were left on the northeast bank. Initially transferred to the *Generalgouvernement*, on 27 April in Jaslo (approx. 400 km northwest of Chotin/*Generalgouvernement*) orders were received for the remains of the brigade to proceed to the SS Training Camp Bohemia.

The remaining elements of the brigade arrived by rail at the SS Training Camp Bohemia on 3 May 1944. On 28 June, during refreshment of the assault brigade, orders were issued for the formation of a second motorized grenadier battalion and the reorganization of the assault gun battery into SS Assault Gun Battalion 56 with three batteries.[33] As all of the battery's assault guns had been lost in the previous action, SS Operational Headquarters ordered that the assault gun battery with eight vehicles intended for the 19th SS Waffen Grenadier Division (Latvian No. 2) be diverted to the 6th SS Volunteer Assault Brigade. The plan to build up the

[33] The number 56 was the result of the general designation of brigade units with a 5 plus the special brigade number. In this case it was 6, therefore 56.

battery into a battalion could not be realized, however, and the brigade's ultimate organization was as follows:

Brigade Headquarters	SS-Sturmbannführer Schellong
I Battalion	SS-Hauptsturmführer Rehmann
1st – 3rd Companies	
4th (Heavy) Company	
5th (Anti-Tank) Company	
II Battalion	SS-Hauptsturmführer Oehms
6th – 8th Companies	
9th (Heavy) Company	
10th (Anti-Tank) Company	SS-Untersturmführer Barrie
Brigade Units	
11th (Infantry Gun) Company	
12th (Assault Gun) Battery	
13th (20-mm Flak) Battery	
14th (88-mm Flak) Battery	

On 30 June 1944 the 6th SS Volunteer Assault Brigade "*Langemarck*" had a reported strength of:

	Officers	NCOs	Enlisted Men	Total
Authorized	47	262	1,422	1,731
	2.72%	15.14%	82.14%	100%
Actual	63	497	1,995	2,555
	2.47%	19.45%	78.08%	100%

As a result of the order for the formation of a second grenadier battalion, the brigade's authorized strength had risen by about 700 men. While these numbers could not be achieved at first, the losses suffered in the previous four months were at least made good by the recruitment of new volunteers. In fact, however, the unit needed a training and regeneration period of about six months before it could become a frontline combat unit.

Notwithstanding this, in mid-July 1944 the unit received orders to form a battle group which was to be sent to the badly battered III SS Panzer Corps in Estonia. On 19 July 1944 a force made up of

Officers	NCOs	Enlisted Men	Total
4	44	195	245
2.5%	18%	79.5%	100%

Jan de Vriese was born in Flanders on 9/8/1925 and in March 1942 joined the Volunteer Legion "*Flanders*".

Remy Schrijnen was born in Flanders on 24/12/1921 and in November 1942 joined the Volunteer Legion "*Flanders*". He was awarded the Knight's Cross of the Iron cross on 21/9/1944.

The members of the Volunteer Legion "*Flanders*" and later the 6th SS Volunteer Assault Brigade "*Langemarck*" wore either the three-armed sun wheel or the usual SS runes on their collar tabs.

under the command of *SS-Hauptsturmführer* Rehmann departed Beneschau in the Protectorate of Bohemia and Moravia by rail. While the III SS Panzer Corps withdrew toward the "Tannenberg Position", on 25 July 1944 the two Flemish companies arrived in the Toila area. The men were immediately sent into action and, together with Estonian troops of the I Battalion, SS Waffen Grenadier Regiment 47 (Estonian No. 3), occupied positions on the so-called "Children's Home Hill". The next day three officers were killed by a shell during a briefing. *SS-Hauptsturmführer* Rehmann was wounded in the hand and made his way to hospital. This resulted in a rumor among the Flemish volunteers that he had fled out of cowardice. *SS-Untersturmführer* D'Haese subsequently assumed command of the battle group. On 28 July the Soviets overran the hill and immediately attacked so-called "Grenadier Hill". *SS-Sturmmann* Schrijnen, gunner on a heavy anti-tank gun, knocked out ten Soviet T 34s and three Josef Stalin heavy tanks. In the end he was serving the gun by himself, having decided to remain instead of flee. For his actions he was awarded the Knight's Cross of the Iron Cross on 21 September 1944. He recalled:

"After I was found to be too short for the Waffen-SS, in 1942, while working in the German armaments industry in Kempten, Allgäu, I volunteered for the mountain infantry. Before I could be called up, in November 1942 the order was issued for the formation of the Flanders Volunteer Legion. After training, I was initially made a runner, but I later became a gunner in the SS Assault Brigade Langemarck's anti-tank company. In the Ukraine on 31 December 1943 we were ordered into action straight from the unloading ramps. There I was able to destroy my first three T 34s. In the spring of 1944, when we became caught up in the 1st Panzer Army pocket, I also engaged enemy field guns that were trying to hinder our retreat. In March 1944 I was wounded and ended up in hospital. I was released in June 1944 and was given four week's convalescent leave. I didn't take it, though. Instead I rejoined my unit, which by then was at Training Camp Milowitz near Prague. In mid-July 1944 I was part of a battle group sent to the Narva bridgehead. Our losses were extremely heavy. The Soviet barrage fire knocked our guns and crews one after another. Finally mine was the only one left and I served it alone! For this I was awarded the Knight's Cross of the Iron Cross. At the end of September 1944 the remnants of our battle group were evacuated to Pomerania aboard the Gotland."

The fighting raged back and forth, and after the Soviets failed to take the German positions they shifted their attacks into the area west of Pskov. On 10 August 1944 the Soviet 3rd Baltic Front attacked the XXVIII Army Corps on the left wing of the 18th Army. On 14 August 1944 Army Detachment Narva, which was tasked with barring the area between Lakes Peipus and Wirz, ordered the commanding officer of the 4th SS Volunteer Grenadier Brigade "*Nederland*", *SS-Brigadeführer* Wagner, to form a battle group to reestablish contact with the XXVIII Army Corps. The remnants of SS Battle Group Rehmann, equivalent to a single company, were attached to Battle Group, 5th SS Volunteer Assault Brigade Wallonien. The Wagner Group consisted of:

I Battalion, SS Waffen Grenadier Regiment 45
I and II Battalions, SS Waffen Grenadier Regiment 46
Grenadier Regiment 23
SS Battle Group "*Wallonien*" with remnants of "*Langemarck*"
SS Armored Reconnaissance Battalion 11
II Battalion, Artillery Regiment 58
III Battalion, Nebelwerfer Regiment 3

Group "Wagner", almost equal in strength to a division, successfully restored contact with the neighboring corps and established a stable front along the Embachs. Nevertheless, near Dorpat the Red Army was able to establish a bridgehead between Lakes Wirz and Peipus.

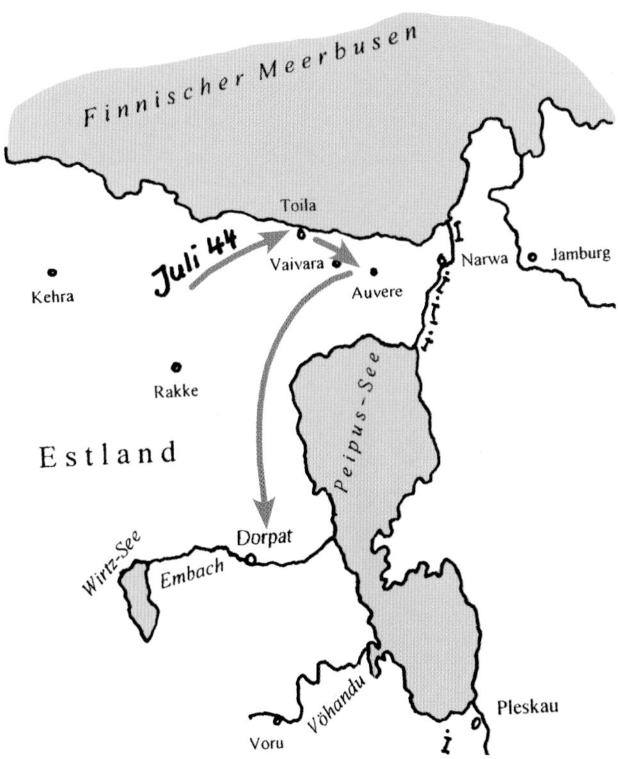

Map: Actions by Brigade "*Rehmann*" in Estonia.

Jan Verneulen joined the 27th SS Volunteer Grenadier Division "*Langemarck*" in 1944 and ultimately served in SS Volunteer Grenadier Regiment 66.

In September 1944 Hitler decided to abandon Estonia. For the Flemish volunteers this first meant a withdrawal to Reval. There, on 19 September, they boarded the ship "Gotland", which arrived in Swinemünde on 25 September. From there the remnants of the battle group marched to SS Training Camp Hammerstein (west of Konitz). On 1 November 1944, SS Battle Group Rehmann boarded trains for transport to Lüneburg Heath for the formation of the 27th SS Volunteer Grenadier Division "*Langemarck*".

The 27th SS Volunteer Grenadier Division "*Langemarck*" (Flemish No. 1)

On 18 September 1944 Himmler decreed that, "*because of the many volunteers, an SS volunteer grenadier division will be formed from the former SS Volunteer Assault Brigade 'Langemarck'.*" As the "*many volunteers*" did not exist at that time, nor indeed could be expected, the question remains why Himmler said this. Goebbels once called him a "realistic politician", so that one can assume that he initiated this farce to possibly deceive the German skeptics in the government and the military, as well as enemy intelligence.

Belgium had already been liberated by the western allies, and the only remaining sources of volunteers were the approximately 19,000 Flemish collaborators (including their families) evacuated to Germany and armaments workers. A lack of enthusiasm for seeing out the war as a member of the *Waffen-SS*, or not seeing it at all, kept interest low. Apart from Flemish youth, who volunteered out of enthusiasm and were concentrated in their own battalion, the new Infantry Division 44 could count few volunteers. As the VNV had stopped supporting recruitment for the *Waffen-SS* in the summer of 1943, almost all of those who joined the *Waffen-SS* were members of DeVlag.

With respect to the formation of the new division, the *Reichsführer-SS* further declared:

"*I select the Lüneburg Heath as the site for formation of the SS Volunteer Grenadier Division 'Langemarck':*

because the majority of the Flemish refugees are being accommodated in the East Hanover district, and thus to some degree this will fill the emptiness of the Lüneburg Heath, which is a tempting target for a parachute drop, because this will spare us making demands of the already overfilled training camps."

On 20 September 1944 the following strength was reported to SS Operational Headquarters:

Officers	NCOs	Enlisted Men	Total	
Actual	46	236	1,659	1,941
2.37%	12.16%	85.47%	100%	
Authorized	433	2,262	9,926	12,621
3.4%	17.9%	78.7%	100%	

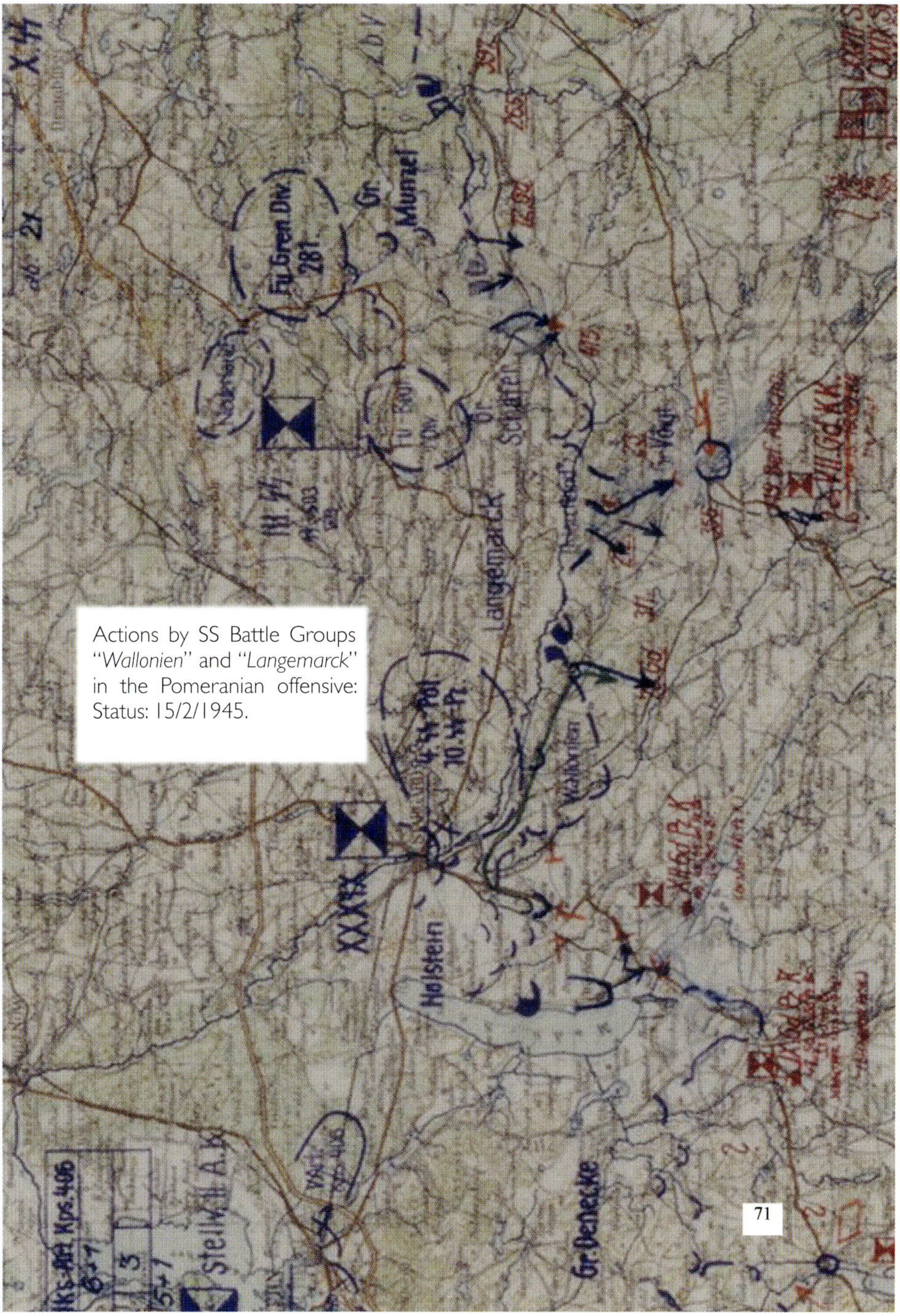

Actions by SS Battle Groups "*Wallonien*" and "*Langemarck*" in the Pomeranian offensive: Status: 15/2/1945.

The division was thus more than 10,000 men below authorized strength. Its planned organization:

Division Headquarters	SS-Standartenführer Müller
SS Volunteer Grenadier Regiment 66 (Flemish No. 1) with two battalions	SS-Obersturmbannführer Schellong
SS Volunteer Grenadier Regiment 67 (Flemish No. 2) with two battalions	SS-Sturmbannführer Hansmann
SS Volunteer Grenadier Regiment 68 (Flemish No. 3) with two battalions	SS-Hauptsturmführer Stange
SS Volunteer Artillery Regiment 27 (Flemish No. 1) with four battalions	SS-Obersturmbannführer Arentoft
SS Pioneer Battalion 27	SS-Hauptsturmführer Bauch
SS Anti-Tank Battalion 27	SS-Hauptsturmführer Wangemann
SS Signals Battalion 27	SS-Hauptsturmführer Krauss
SS Medical Battalion 27	SS-Sturmbannführer Dr. Tieltgens
SS-Division Fusilier Battalion 27	
SS Field Replacement Battalion 27	
SS Supply Regiment 27	

During October 1944 the division, which was sometimes called the Volks-Grenadier Division "*Langemarck*" for recruiting purposes, received its first recruits. After about 10 weeks of training, they were sworn in in mid-December. Most units, however, such as SS Volunteer Grenadier Regiment 68 and SS-Division Fusilier Battalion 27, could not be established because of a shortage of personnel.

Just before Christmas 1944 a regiment-strength battle group was formed under the command of *SS-Obersturmbannführer* Schellong, commander of the SS Volunteer Grenadier Regiment 66, consisting of:

I Battalion, SS Volunteer Grenadier Regiment 66,
I Battalion, SS Volunteer Grenadier Regiment 67 and
SS Anti-Tank Battalion 27[34].

The roughly 2,000 men were transported by rail to Cologne-Wahn, arriving there on 24 December 1944. From there the men marched into the area of the Urftal dam (Fore Eifel). As the Flemish volunteers were fundamentally intended for employment on the Eastern Front, SS Battle Group Schellong was only supposed to guard the area, thus freeing up German troops. The move was almost certainly also intended to deceive enemy intelligence.

---

[34] The battalion was formed from the previous heavy battalion and brigade units.

Far away, on 18 January 1945 orders arrived for the unit to be reorganized as an Infantry Division 45, so that it could at least come close to reaching its authorized strength. The former commander of SS Panzer Grenadier Regiment 20, *SS-Standartenführer* Müller, was placed in command of the division. His task was to complete the formation of the division in Soltau with a minimized organization in men and materiel. Although actual strength had risen by about 2,000 men to approximately 4,000, even in its new abbreviated form the unit was still short approximately 5,000 men.

Meanwhile, the Red Army had launched a major offensive on 12 January 1945, and within a few days had brought the German Eastern Front to collapse. As Hitler forbade the transfer of the 6th SS Panzer Army from the west or the army fighting in the Courland to Pomerania, beginning on 21 January 1945 Army Group Vistula was hastily formed. Four days later *Reichsführer-SS* Himmler was named its commander-in-chief, with orders to close the approximately 150-kilometer gap in the front between the 9th Army and the newly-to-be-created 11th Army (Army Group Vistula) between Glogau and Elbing. And so for just under two months, a man who had never attended an officer's school or completed a course for senior commanders would be the commander-in-chief of an army group.

During the reinforcement of the 11th Army and preparations for a German offensive, at the end of January 1945 the Commander-in-Chief West shifted a number of units from the Fore-Eifel to Pomerania, including SS Battle Group Schellong. Sent to the III (Germanic) SS Panzer Corps, at the beginning of February 1945 it arrived in the area west of Ravenstein. On 16 February 1945 a joint attack was to be launched by Himmler in Pomerania and *Generaloberst* Schörner in Silesia, which was to destroy the Red Army forces that had advanced to the Oder. The 11th Army was organized as follows:

Acting Corps Headquarters, II Army Corps (General der Infanterie Hörnlein)
- 9th Parachute Division
- Generalleutnant Denecke Group (elements of Division No. 471)

XXXIX Panzer Corps (General der Panzertruppen Decker)
- Panzer Division[35] "Holstein" (from the 233rd Reserve Panzer Division)
- 4th SS Police Panzer Grenadier Division
- 10th SS Panzer Division "Frundsberg"
- SS Battle Group "Wallonien"

III (Germanic) SS Panzer Corps (Generalleutnant Unrein)
- 11th SS Volunteer Panzer Grenadier Division "Nordland"
- 23rd SS Volunteer Panzer Grenadier Division "Nederland"
- SS Battle Group "Langemarck"

[35] In fact, it was only a panzer grenadier division, which also had a serious shortage of anti-tank weapons.

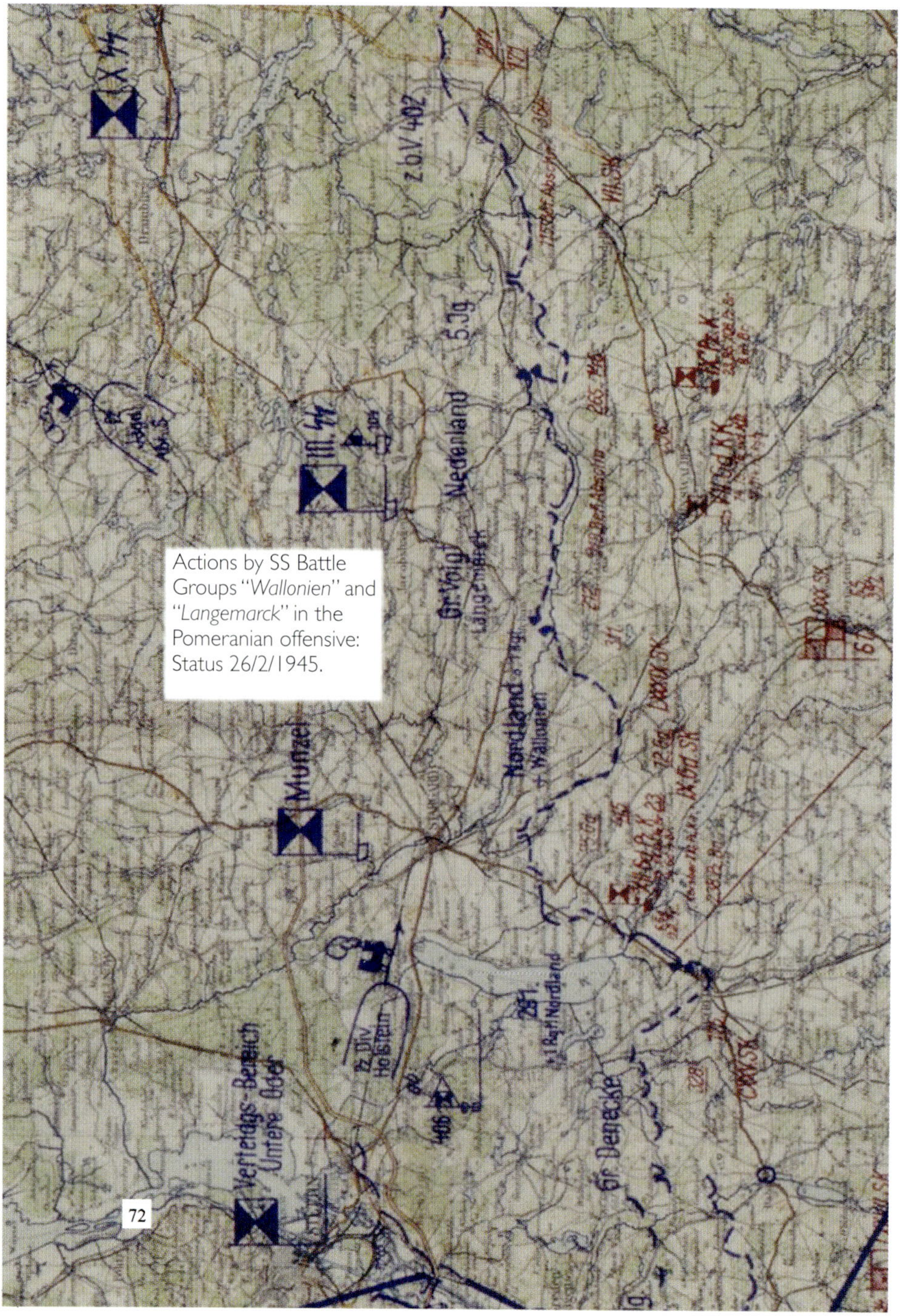

Actions by SS Battle Groups "*Wallonien*" and "*Langemarck*" in the Pomeranian offensive: Status 26/2/1945.

Munzel Group[36] (Generalmajor Munzel)
Führer Escort Division
Gruppe Grenadier Division
X SS Army Corps (Generalleutnant Krappe)
Special Purpose Division 402 (replacement units from Defense District II)
Group from the 5th Light Infantry Division
Oberst Lehmann Group (officer candidates from Artillery School II)
"Tettau" Corps (Generalleutnant von Tettau) from Headquarters, Special Purpose Division 604
Action Division "Köslin"[37] from units of the Defense Replacement Inspectorate Köslin
Action Division "Bärwalde" made up of officer candidates from Artillery School II and Volkssturm

With no air support and inadequate artillery preparation, the offensive barely had a chance to unfold. The troops—whether grenadiers or panzer grenadiers—were halted by the bottomless, muddy roads and Soviet tanks. Together with elements of the 11th and 23rd SS Volunteer Panzer Grenadier Divisions, the Flemish volunteers attacked toward encircled Arnswalde and guarded the attack force's right wing in the area Petznick – Schönwerder (approx. 12 km northwest of Arnswalde). After seven tanks and an armored troop carrier broke straight into the city on 16 February, two days later the 11th SS Volunteer Panzer Grenadier Division "*Nordland*" drove through to the north edge of Arnswalde and was able to hold a corridor with a maximum width of 1.5 kilometers. On 19 February the evacuation of the approximately 7,000 civilians—on foot—through the corridor began. On the evening of 21 February 1945, the survivors of the battle group under the command of *Generalmajor* Voigt followed, unnoticed by the Soviets.

As the other units of the 11th Army made little progress and with Soviet resistance growing steadily stronger, "Operation Solstice" was called off in order to avoid the "*pointless wastage of the attacking units*". Thus, the ambitious Pomeranian operation ended after about five days. Its greatest success was the drive into encircled Arnswalde, about 10 kilometers distant. After the attacking units withdrew to the original main line of resistance behind the Ohna, the Red Army pushed forward and established several small bridgeheads across the river.

---

[36] The "Menzel" Group consisted of 2 Volkssturm battalions, elements of the Escort Battalion "*Reichsführer-SS*", Anti-Tank Battalion 104, the "Stargard" and "von den Groeben" Alert Battalions plus Cavalry Training Battalion 100 from Stolp, Armored Train Platoon 77, and Armored Train Instruction Platoon 5. After the withdrawal of the XXXIX Panzer Corps, Group Headquarters "Munzel" was reorganized as Corps Headquarters "Munzel".

[37] The Action Division was renamed "*Pommernland*" in February 1945.

Actions by the Flemings and Wallonians in Division Group "*Müller*" of the Oder Corps. Status: 19/4/1945.

Battle Group "*Langemarck*" took part in fierce fighting in the area Zachan – Schwanenbeck (approx. 20 km southeast of Stargard).

Several days later, on 1 March 1945, the Soviets launched their own offensive, resulting in extremely fierce fighting in the Stargard – Zachan area. Battle Group "*Langemarck*" moved via Seefeld (approx. 5 km northwest of Stargard) into the area around Altdamm, which was envisaged as a bridgehead. There it was attached to the XXXII Army Corps near Hökendorf, together with the remnants of the Wallonian SS battle group. After several days of rest, on 15 March the Red Army attacked the bridgehead position after drum fire from massed artillery and tanks. Four days later Hitler approved the abandonment of the area, which was originally supposed to be the jumping-off point for a German offensive in the direction of Danzig. The last German troops left the bridgehead on 20 March 1945.

The remains of Battle Group "*Langemarck*" subsequently moved into the Prenzlau area. In the past six weeks the battle group had lost far in excess of half of its men, and only about 600 arrived in the new quartering area. At the same time, in Soltau *SS-Standartenführer* Müller received orders to move the elements of the division not yet committed out of the Lüneburg Heath to Prenzlau, out of the way of the advancing Allies. On 6 April 1945 the unit submitted the following strength report:

	Officers	NCOs	Enlisted Men	Total
Actual	167	408	3,527	4,102
	4.07%	9.95%	85.98%	100%

After more than half a year the shortfall of about 4,000 men below the authorized strength of a 1945 Infantry Division could not be made good. The intake of new volunteers was only sufficient to make good the losses in killed and severely wounded. The Commander-in-Chief of the 3rd Panzer Army, *General der Panzertruppen* von Manteuffel, made the following assessment of the Flemish SS unit at that time:

"*The division is only a regiment-size group with two strong battalions and a heavy battalion with heavy infantry guns and three heavy anti-tank guns. The division has good men but bad officers. Unsuitable for offensive tasks, only for defense, in this case artillery support is desirable.*"

At the same time the 27th SS Volunteer Grenadier Division "*Langemarck*" reported having:

120 light and 20 heavy machine-guns
4 medium 81.4-mm mortars
4 light and 2 heavy infantry guns
6 light and 4 heavy field howitzers
41 field kitchens
22 motorcycles
26 automobiles
41 trucks
2 prime movers
300 horses

At least the armament for the fighting troops could be characterized as adequate. After assembling his unit, on 15 April 1945 *SS-Standartenführer* Müller received an order from the 3rd Panzer Army directing him to take command of a mixed Belgian division group. This was to be created from elements of the 27th and 28th SS Volunteer Grenadier Divisions and bolstered by other units, including Anti-Tank Battalion 6 and the assault battalion of the 3rd Panzer Army. Attached to *SS-Obergruppenführer* von dem Bach's Oder Corps as counterattack reserve, the division group was assembled in the Damitzow – Pomellen – Hohenholz area. It consisted of:

I Battalion, SS Volunteer Grenadier Regiment 66 (Flemish No. 1)
SS Volunteer Grenadier Regiment 67 (Flemish No. 2)
2 mixed batteries, SS Volunteer Artillery Regiment 27
SS Volunteer Grenadier Regiment 69 (Wallonian No. 1)
Anti-Tank Battalion 6
Assault Battalion, 3rd Panzer Army

Tactically, the two battalions of SS Volunteer Grenadier Regiment 67 were attached to the adjoining group of forces on the right under Oberst Wellmann.

On 20 April 1945 the 2nd White Russian Front also initiated offensive activities in the Oder Corps' area. After the Soviets established a bridgehead south of Stettin, the Belgian SS volunteers saw action in the Kolbitzow – Schillersdorf – Tantow area. The units were deployed separately, with the Walloons in particular fighting alongside Special Purpose Division 610 and finally being squeezed into the Brüssow area, while the Flemings attached to *Oberst* Wellmann's group were forced to withdraw via Penkun toward Prenzlau. Running along the marshy Randow Valley, the Wotan Position played no part in the defense. With no combat-capable units left in that sector, the Belgians, too, were caught up in the rapidly-developing cases of disintegration (especially among Hungarian and Rumanian "volunteers").

After the Oder Corps' headquarters was dissolved, SS Battle Group "*Langemarck*" was attached to the XXXXVI Panzer Corps, and on 25 April 1945 was deployed in front of Breslau. The situation was stabilized somewhat after additional units of the 27th SS Volunteer Grenadier Division were sent. The arrival of additional units (including SS Pioneer Battalion 27, sent to the Eastern Front from the SS Pioneer School in Hradischko; II Battalion, SS Volunteer Grenadier Regiment 67, made up of Flemish youth; or SS Anti-Tank Battalion 27) was not enough to prevent the Red Army from taking Prenzlau on 27 April 1945.

That same day *General der Panzertruppen* von Manteuffel, commander-in-chief of the 3rd Panzer Army, gave a vivid description of the situation:

"*Complete disintegration of the units 'Langemarck', 'Wallonien', 1st Marine Division and all of the anti-aircraft battalions, insofar as they lost their weapons through their own fault or not. I didn't witness such scenes as this even in 1918. All that remains of the "Langemarck" Division and the 1st Marine Division are their brave commanders and a number of people over whom they have retained command through voice and heart...*"

The next day the XXXXVI Panzer Corps occupied positions in the lake-rich area between Strasburg and Lychen. From left to right in the main line of resistance were the remnants of the:

281st Infantry Division
SS Battle Group "Wallonien"
SS Panzer Grenadier Regiment 7 with SS Battle Group "Solar"
Panzer Training Unit "Ostsee"
SS Battle Group "Langemarck"
1st Marine Division

Legion "*Wallonie*" postcards.

On the right: Leutnant Degrelle.

The Flemish SS volunteers saw action near Feldberg, and by the following day withdrew toward Neustrelitz. By way of Waren, which they reached on 30 April, the volunteers marched through Karow, and on 2 May 1945 became prisoners of the western allies. Initially concentrated in the POW camp in Fallingbostel, the Flemings were returned to Belgium in several transports, and by the end of 1946 had been handed over to Belgian authorities. Thus ended their war service on the German side.

The volunteers from Flanders, most of whom did not want to serve in the SS, were always committed at the hotspots of the Eastern Front. As a result, they suffered a much higher rate of loss than other units of the *Waffen-SS* or army. Convinced supporters of the struggle against communism, this almost insignificant element of the Belgian population did not disappoint the German command. The signs of disintegration among the Flemish troops at the end of April 1945 may have been more marked because they faced a more uncertain future than was the case for the German troops.

28th SS Volunteer Grenadier Division "*Wallonien*" (Wallonian No. 1)

The Legion "*Wallonie*"

Like the Volunteer Legion "*Flandern*", the Wallonian volunteer legion was created primarily for propaganda reasons. Hitler wanted to emphasize the common European struggle against communism by establishing western European volunteer legions. "Operation Barbarossa" was supposed to be a "**quick campaign**" lasting about four months, and as originally planned this participation was purely theoretical. Even by taking in already trained foreign soldiers, the formation and training of volunteer units required three to four months. By then, however, the war against the Soviet Union would already be over.

In the course of this agitation there were also negotiations with Wallonian politicians. Leading the way was Leon Degrelle, leader of the *Parti Populaire de Rex*, who hoped that participation by members of his party in the war against Bolshevism would enhance his position after Germany's final victory.

Recruitment among Degrelle's Rexists was relatively well received. In keeping with Hitler's "*Guidelines for the Use of Foreign Volunteers in the Struggle against the Soviet Union*", at first all volunteers were accepted. The actual physical examinations were held in the so-called "Camp Earthworm" near Meseritz. Numerous older men and younger ones unfit for military service who had volunteered for the Wallonian Infantry Battalion 373 were rejected as unsuitable.

Formation of a unit in the late summer of 1941 was not unproblematic, as the German military was not prepared to train and employ foreigners. Language problems, different mentality, and sharply differing standards of training among serving Belgian soldiers could only be alleviated to a certain degree in the short term.

Trained or retrained according to German rules, on 17 October 1941 the Legion "*Wallonie*", with a strength of 19 officers and 850 other ranks, was loaded onto trains for transport to the Eastern Front. On 2 November, about four months after the start of the war, they arrived in Dnepropetrovsk. Initially the unit continued training close to the front. On 26 January 1942, after the Soviets launched their winter offensive, the unit was sent to the front in the 100th Light Infantry Division's sector. The Walloons were then deployed in the Gromova Balka area (approx. 40 km southwest of Kramatorowka) together with a battalion of Croatian Infantry Regiment 369 and I Battalion, SS-Regiment "*Germania*". After the extraordinarily fierce and costly fighting, the remnants of Infantry Battalion 373 were sent to Blagodat, a few kilometers away, to rest and reequip. It was by then obvious that the planned blitzkrieg campaign against the Soviet Union had failed.

The Legion "*Wallonie*" during refurbishment at Training Camp Meseritz in the spring of 1943.

Center: Hauptmann Lippert
To his right: Leutnant Degrelle

While in Brussels a new contingent of Wallonian volunteers was leaving for training at Camp Earthworm, in the east there were further fierce defensive battles from the end of February to the beginning of March 1942. Decimated in the fighting, the Legion was again rested and reequipped in Blagodat. On 5 May 1943 the Legion "*Wallonie*" was attached to the 97th Light Infantry Division and ordered into the Slavyansk area. Bolstered by replacements from Meseritz that arrived on 2 June 1942, on 22 June, as part of the German summer offensive, the battalion crossed the Donets south of Izyum and marched in a southeasterly arc to Shakhty. Meeting no serious resistance, the Wallonians arrived in the Maykop area on 18 August. They had covered nearly 1,000 kilometers in just under two months. This was followed by an unsuccessful advance toward Tuapse, about 100 kilometers away in a straight line. After heavy fighting—including near Cheryakov (approx. 60 km southwest of Maykop)—in mid-November the Legion "*Wallonie*" was relieved and transferred to the training camp near Meseritz. With the exception of a company of Wallonian volunteers, who had only been called up in March 1942 and remained in the Caucasus, in mid-December 1942 the men of Wallonian Infantry Battalion 373 were given three weeks home leave.

On 17 January 1943 in the Brussels Sports Palace, the Legion "*Wallonie*" was given an official farewell as it departed for the Eastern Front for the second time. First, however, the men were sent to the training camp near Meseritz. There the veteran volunteers were to be joined with the recruits to form a capable operational unit.

Map: Actions by the Wallonian Infantry Battalion 373.

The 5th SS Volunteer Assault Brigade "*Wallonien*"

The first discussions between *SS-Gruppenführer* Berger, chief of SS Headquarters, and Degrelle about transferring the Legion "*Wallonie*" to the *Waffen-SS* took place in December 1942. Degrelle, who hoped to get more support for the Wallonian volunteers from the SS than he had from the *Wehrmacht*, agreed to the transfer.

On 17 January 1943, during a speech at the Brussels Sports Palace, Degrelle informed the surprised listeners that the Walloons were entirely German. The first propaganda step for the transfer of the Wallonian volunteers into the *Waffen-SS* had been taken.

He followed the same propaganda line in a speech to several thousand Belgian and French armaments workers in the Berlin Sports Palace on 31 January 1943. Ultimately about 100 of the Frenchmen volunteered for the assault brigade. There followed personal discussions with Himmler. It is interesting that he negotiated, not with *Hauptmann* Lippert, commander of the Wallonian Infantry Battalion 373, but with *Leutnant* Degrelle, who saw himself as the Wallonian racial leader. After the two days of talks, on 24 May 1943 the *Reichsführer-SS* visited the Wallonian volunteers in Meseritz. Himmler later noted:

"*After discussions with the OKW and agreement on the part of General Zeitzler, Chief of the Army General Staff, I have decided to incorporate the Wallonian Legion into the Waffen-SS as a Germanic volunteer legion.*

The political path taken by the Rexist leader Leon Degrelle over the years was logically-pursued and correct. In each case he selected the forms which were undoubtedly the right ones for his Wallonian people, a positive building of strength of a renewing kind. Throughout the past year I watched as the "pan Germanics" were labeled and those Reichsleiter so disposed put out feelers to Degrelle and his party. I merely dismissed the man and his movement, which was not as advanced then. In 1941, therefore, when the legion was being formed, I rejected its incorporation into the Waffen-SS.

After the legion's outstanding performance on the Eastern Front which, in contrast to the Belgian Army's past, earned the esteem and respect of the German soldiers, as a result of his experience at the front the right time came when, in his great speech at the beginning of the year, he was able to declare to the Walloons that they were a Germanic tribe by history and ancestry, Romanized in language and culture. After this step had been taken by the Rexist leader Degrelle and his movement, it was up to me, having been made responsible by the Führer for perceiving all Germanic questions, to recognize the legion as a Germanic fighting unit and the movement in Wallonia as the renewing movement of an essentially Germanic people."

Above: *SS-Brigadeführer* Vahl, Inspector of *Waffen-SS* Armored Forces. To his left is *SS-Obersturmführer* Reich.
Right: *Hauptmann* Lippert, commander of the Legion "*Wallonie*".

Reichsführer-SS Himmler inspects the Legion "*Wallonie*" on 24 May 1943. Right: *Hauptmann* Lippert.

Hauptmann Lippert presents officers of the Legion "*Wallonie*".

SS Gruppenführer Berger (on the right, beside Himmler), Chief of SS Headquarters, was also present at the inspection.

The core was formed by the approximately 700 members of Wallonian Infantry Battalion 373. In Belgium, Degrelle appealed for men to join the SS Volunteer Assault Brigade "*Wallonien*", including in the party newspaper *L'Avenir*. The call to join the armored SS Volunteer Assault Brigade "*Wallonien*" was supposed to show propagandistically to the Belgians and the world the type of military technology Germany possessed in the fourth year of the war. All men between the ages of 17 and 40 who were at least 1.65 meters tall could volunteer. Those accepted had to sign a commitment to serve until the war was over. The bulk of the volunteers came from the Rexist movement. Recruiting in Belgium and among the armaments workers in Germany produced about 900 volunteers for the *Waffen-SS*. Given that there were about three-million Walloons, it is a number that speaks for itself!

Under the command of former battalion commander Lippert, since promoted to *SS-Sturmbannführer*, on 27 June 1943 the Walloons were transferred to Training Camp Wildflecken for further training. Training of the supporting arms units was initially carried out at the respective schools. As the unit's strength did not exceed about 1,600 men, however, it was to be organized as a "new type" assault brigade. This meant the formation of:

Brigade Headquarters	SS-Sturmbannführer Lippert
Headquarters Company	SS-Obersturmführer van Oldruytenborg
1st Company	SS-Obersturmführer Mathieu
2nd Company	SS-Obersturmführer Derriks
3rd Company	SS-Obersturmführer Degrelle
4th Company	SS-Untersturmführer Bonniver
5th (Anti-Tank) Company	SS-Untersturmführer Lamproye
6th (20-mm Flak) Company	SS-Obersturmführer Calonne
7th (88-mm Flak) Company	SS-Untersturmführer Dumont
8th (Inf. Gun) Company	SS-Untersturmführer Graff
9th (Assault Gun) Company	SS-Untersturmführer Dengis
10th (Supply) Company	SS-Untersturmführer Ruelle

And so a unit that never reached regiment strength was given the misleading designation of SS Volunteer Brigade.

On 17 October 1943 the Red Army launched a major offensive across the Dniepr, and at the beginning of November the Wallonian volunteers in Wildflecken were placed on alert. After four months—before the planned training date—they were sent to the Eastern Front. The unit, which was equipped with about 300 vehicles and trained for winter fighting, was transported by rail to the area west of Cherkassy. There it was attached to the III Panzer Corps. While the bulk of the brigade was deployed in the main line of resistance in the Mozhny – Baibusy

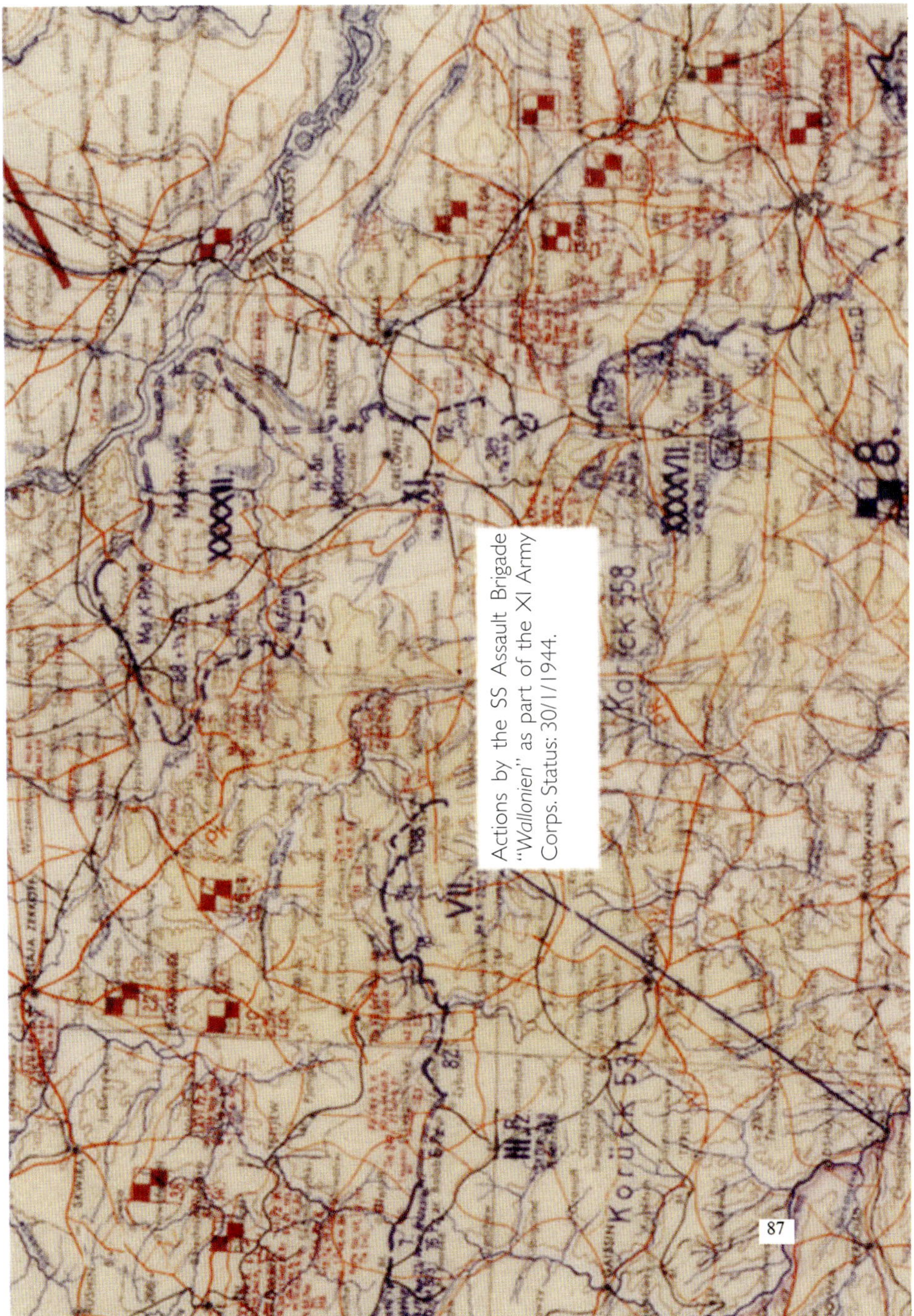

Actions by the SS Assault Brigade "*Wallonien*" as part of the XI Army Corps. Status: 30/1/1944.

area beginning 20 November 1943, about 300 volunteers with just four months of training behind them were employed in an anti-partisan role in the Irdyn area (approx. 4 km west of Cherkassy). Many suspected partisans were shot during this time.

The brigade's reported strength on 1 January 1944:

	Officers	NCOs	Enlisted Men	Total
Actual	26	226	1,596	1,848
	1.41%	12.23%	86.36%	100%
Authorized	59	346	1,562	1,967
	3%	17.6%	79.4%	100%

Of these, about 1,600 were at the front. The rest, approximately 250 recently inducted volunteers, were still at the training camp in Wildflecken. At that time the brigade was relatively well-equipped and had available the following equipment and weapons:

10 assault guns
9 75-mm anti-tank guns
118 trucks, 16 of them capable of off-road use
18 Raupenschlepper Ost (RSO)
66 motorcycles, 35 with sidecars
68 automobiles

At the beginning of January 1944 the brigade saw further action against partisans in the rear area, as well as in the Staroselye – Olshana area. On 25 January 1944 the Red Army launched a major offensive, and three days later encircled about 56,000 men of the XI and XXXXII Army Corps west of Cherkassy. The Belgian formation, by then part of XI Army Corps and renamed 5th SS Volunteer Assault Brigade "*Wallonien*" since 22 October 1943, was also affected. As a result of the encirclement, the XXXXII Army Corps had to hurriedly face its front to the north and northwest and the XI Army Corps to the south and southwest. The Russians launched heavy attacks in an attempt to quickly split the pocket. There was heavy fighting for possession of Korsun, the only airfield in the pocket and the supply base for the encircled troops.

Attempts to relieve the approximately 2,500-square-kilometer pocket from the outside failed. On 9 February the German formations abandoned large areas of the pocket in the south, southeast, east and northeast, and moved the troops in a westerly direction. Ultimately the encircled troops were squeezed into an area around Shanderovka about 15 square kilometers in size. After it became obvious that a fresh relief attempt would not succeed, on 16 February Hitler approved a

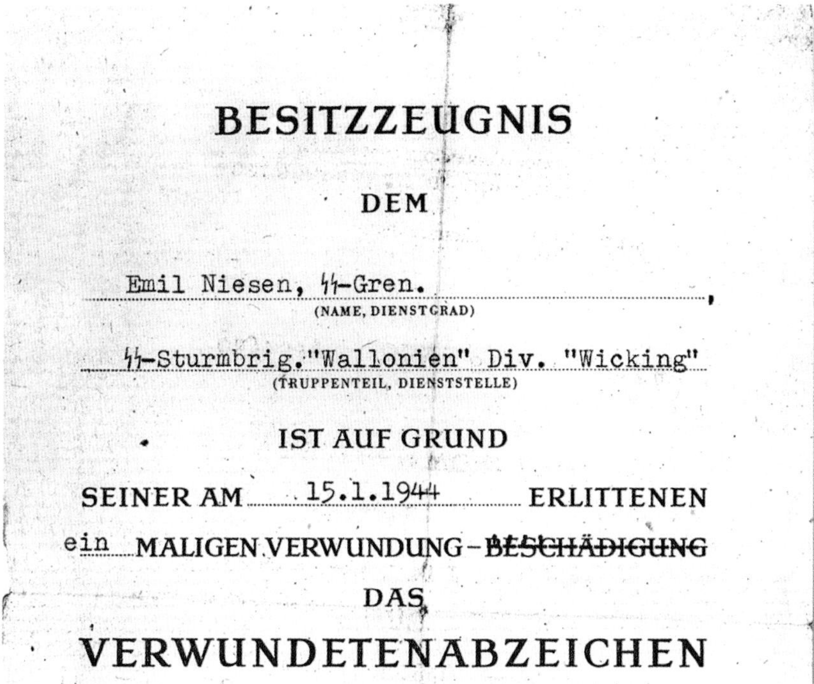

BESITZZEUGNIS

DEM

Emil Niesen, ᛋᛋ-Gren.,
(NAME, DIENSTGRAD)

ᛋᛋ-Sturmbrig. "Wallonien" Div. "Wicking"
(TRUPPENTEIL, DIENSTSTELLE)

IST AUF GRUND

SEINER AM 15.1.1944 ERLITTENEN

ein MALIGEN VERWUNDUNG – ~~BESCHÄDIGUNG~~

DAS

VERWUNDETENABZEICHEN

IN Schwarz

VERLIEHEN WORDEN.

Chyrow, , DEN 6.3. 1944

rzt i. V.

E)

Emil Niesen was wounded near Cherkassy on 15/1/1944.

Emil Niesen was born in the Wallonian province of Luxemburg on 22/12/1923 and joined the SS Assault Brigade "*Wallonien*" in the spring of 1943.

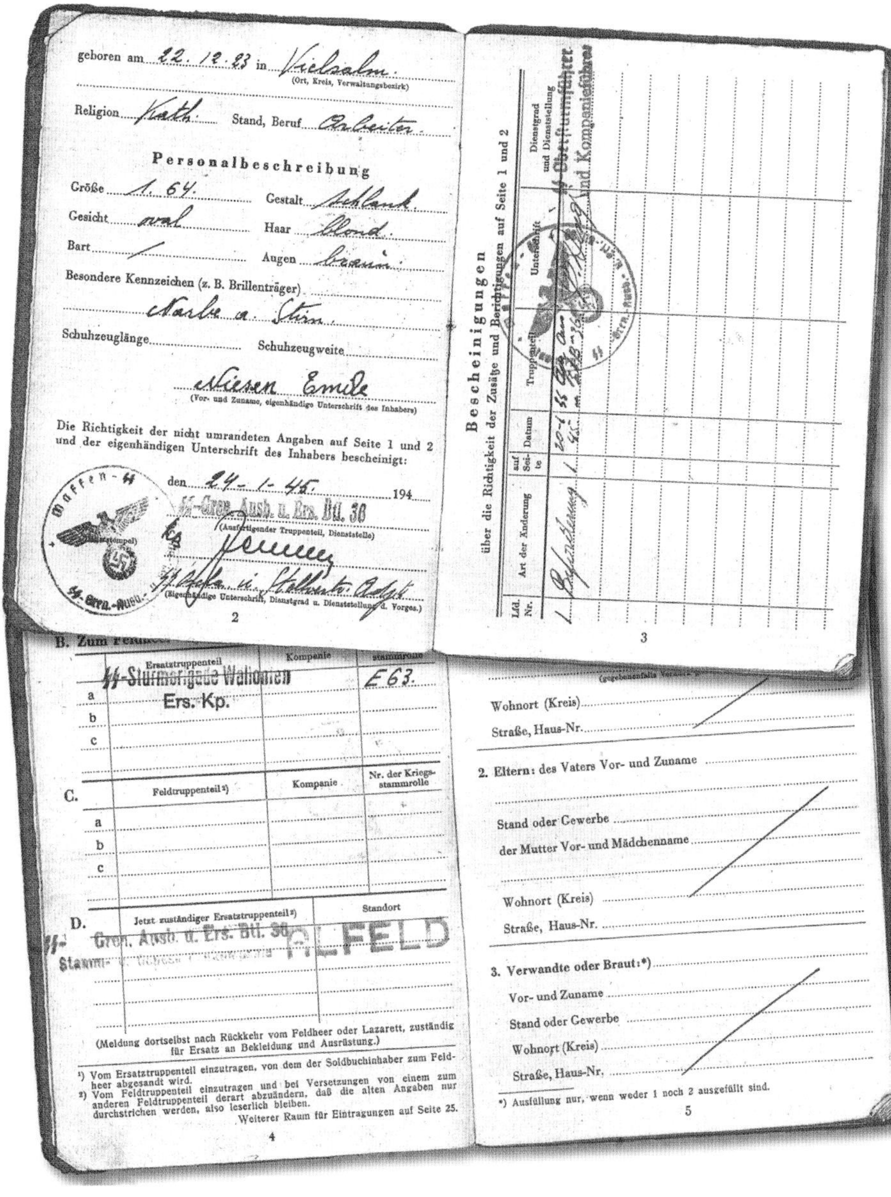
geboren am 22. 12. 23 in Vielsalm.
(Ort, Kreis, Verwaltungsbezirk)
Religion Kath. Stand, Beruf Arbeiter.

Personalbeschreibung

Größe 1. 64. Gestalt schlank.
Gesicht oval Haar blond.
Bart / Augen braun.
Besondere Kennzeichen (z. B. Brillenträger)
Narbe a. Stirn.
Schuhzeuglänge Schuhzeugweite
Niesen Emile
(Vor- und Zuname, eigenhändige Unterschrift des Inhabers)

Die Richtigkeit der nicht umrandeten Angaben auf Seite 1 und 2 und der eigenhändigen Unterschrift des Inhabers bescheinigt:

den 24. 1. 45. 194
SS-Gren. Ausb. u. Ers. Btl. 36
(Ausfertigender Truppenteil, Dienststelle)
(Eigenhändige Unterschrift, Dienstgrad u. Dienststellung d. Vorges.)

2

Bescheinigungen über die Richtigkeit der Zusätze und Berichtigungen auf Seite 1 und 2

Lfd. Nr.	Art der Änderung	auf Seite	Datum	Truppenteil	Unterschrift	Dienstgrad und Dienststellung
1.	Befördertung	1.	20.1.45.			SS-Obersturmführer und Kompanieführer

3

B. Zum Feldheer

	Ersatztruppenteil	Kompanie	Stammrolle
	SS-Sturmbrigade Wallonien Ers. Kp.		E 63.
a			
b			
c			

C.	Feldtruppenteil 2)	Kompanie	Nr. der Kriegsstammrolle
a			
b			
c			

D.	Jetzt zuständiger Ersatztruppenteil 1)	Standort
	SS-Gren. Ausb. u. Ers. Btl. 36	ALFELD

(Meldung dortselbst nach Rückkehr vom Feldheer oder Lazarett, zuständig für Ersatz an Bekleidung und Ausrüstung.)

1) Vom Ersatztruppenteil einzutragen, von dem der Soldbuchinhaber zum Feldheer abgesandt wird.
2) Vom Feldtruppenteil einzutragen und bei Versetzungen von einem zum anderen Feldtruppenteil derart abzuändern, daß die alten Angaben nur durchstrichen werden, also leserlich bleiben.
Weiterer Raum für Eintragungen auf Seite 25.

4

Wohnort (Kreis)
Straße, Haus-Nr.
2. Eltern: des Vaters Vor- und Zuname
Stand oder Gewerbe
der Mutter Vor- und Mädchenname
Wohnort (Kreis)
Straße, Haus-Nr.
3. Verwandte oder Braut: *)
Vor- und Zuname
Stand oder Gewerbe
Wohnort (Kreis)
Straße, Haus-Nr.
*) Ausfüllung nur, wenn weder 1 noch 2 ausgefüllt sind.

5

After he was wounded near Cherkassy, Niesen was assigned to the SS Grenadier Training and Replacement Battalion 36. Then, at the beginning of 1945, he was transferred to the replacement company of the SS Assault Brigade "*Wallonien*".

On 1 April 1944 the 5th SS Assault Brigade "*Wallonien*" returned to Belgium after its action at Cherkassy to great propaganda fanfare. In Cherleroi it was welcomed home by *SS Gruppenführer* Jungclaus, the Reichsführer-SS' Plenipotentiary in Belgium, and *SS Obergruppenführer* Dittrich.

breakout to the west by the trapped divisions. The breakout began on the night of 17 February, and the 5th SS Volunteer Assault Brigade "*Wallonien*" was one of the screening units in the Novo Buda sector. After the original plan of driving straight for Lysyanka failed due to powerful Soviet tank units and the shortage of heavy weapons, the German troops withdrew to the south. There they crossed the Gnilio Tikich, several meters wide with drifting ice in places, under heavy enemy fire using improvised bridges or swimming. Many wounded and non-swimmers drowned there.

Beyond the river, about 35,000 soldiers in their stiff, frozen uniforms reached the forward positions of the III Panzer Corps and were directed north to Lysyanka. Of the original approximately 1,600 Walloons, just 232 were in the reception area west of Uman on 26 February 1944. Fernand Kaisergruber, then an *SS-Unterscharführer*, remembered:

"*I was born near Antwerp on 18 January 1923. As I wanted to stand up for a new order in Europe without Bolshevism, on 3 November 1941 I joined the Wallonian Guard. From there, in the spring of 1943 I and some of my comrades volunteered to serve in Wallonian Infantry Battalion 373. In June 1943 we were automatically transferred to the Waffen-SS. The breakout from the Cherkassy Pocket was dramatic. We ran toward the west, practically with only what we could carry! There was little semblance of order left—in some respects the breakout resembled a Götterdämmerung. One can perhaps so characterize the apocalypse. Badly wounded on 17 February 1944, I was in recovery for more than a year and did not see action again until 22 March 1945 in Pomerania.*"

The transfer of the remaining Wallonian SS volunteers back to Training Camp Wildflecken started at the beginning of March 1944. To exploit the propaganda value of the 5th SS Volunteer Assault Brigade *Wallonien*'s actions, and at the same time show that the German units had come out of the Cherkassy Pocket unbroken, the volunteers were given three weeks home leave. *SS-Sturmbannführer* Degrelle, now the brigade's commander, very effectively stage-managed the return of the Wallonian Eastern Front volunteers. On 28 March the Walloons arrived at the Belgian training camp in Beverloo (approx. 25 km southwest of Neerpelt) from Wildflecken. There the 12th SS Panzer Division "*Hitlerjugend*" provided them with armored troop carriers and drivers, and on 2 April 1944 they paraded through Brussels, about 70 kilometers away, like victorious home comers.

At the end of April 1944 the Wallonian SS volunteers were transferred to SS Training Camp Heidelager, near Debica, for reformation. Thanks to his demagogic appearances, until the summer of 1944 Degrelle was able to recruit about 800 volunteers for the assault brigade, mainly Wallonians working in the German

SS-Obersturmführer Degrelle presents each of the newly-created elements of the SS Volunteer Assault Brigade "*Wallonien*" with a flag of the Wallonian resistance movement. Center photo: note that the SS-*Unterscharführer* in the front is wearing plain black collar patches. Actually a special patch bearing the Burgundy Cross was supposed to have been introduced, but in fact later only sigrunen were worn.

armaments industry (mostly members of the Rexists) and Frenchmen. Recruitment took time, and on 30 June 1944 the brigade reported a strength of:

	Officers	NCOs	Enlisted Men	Total
Actual	53	232	903	1,188
	4.46%	19.53%	76.01%	100%
Authorized	64	497	1,996	2,557
	2.5%	19.44%	78.6%	100%

If one adds to the 250 Walloons still in Germany the approximately 630 returning from action on the Eastern Front, one can see that only about 300 new recruits could be inducted by the end of June 1944.

On 16 July 1944 the brigade received orders to form a battle group, which was to be sent to Army Detachment Narva in Estonia. Designated Battle Group/ SS Volunteer Assault Brigade "*Wallonien*" and made up of two grenadier and one heavy companies, plus an anti-tank platoon (total of 440 men), it was attached to

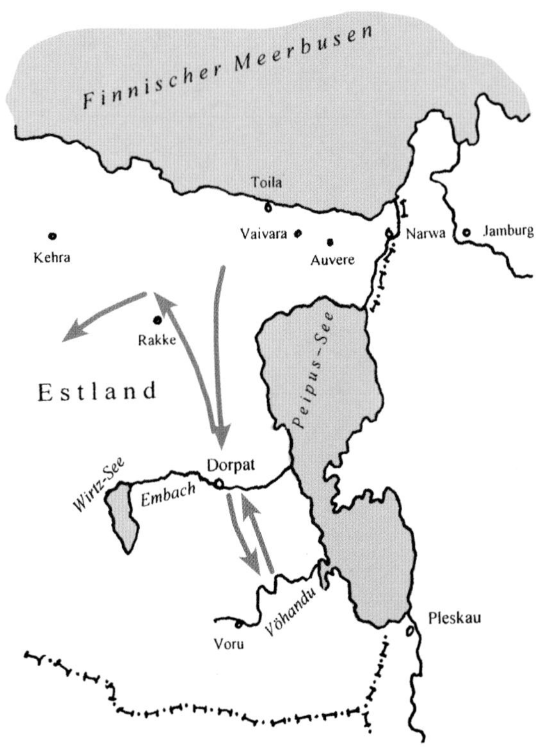

Map: Actions by the Wallonian SS Battle Group in Estonia.

Wildflecken: new recruits are sworn in. They ranged in age from 17 to 45 years.

the division-strength SS Brigade "*Wagner*" (III (Germanic) Panzer Corps) in the Vaivara area. The SS battle group was supposed to restore contact with the XXXXIII Army Corps, part of the 16th Army, a gap of several kilometers having resulted from the Soviet thrust south of Lake Pskov. By way of a temporary intermediate position along the Ahya River, the units occupied the Embach River line around Dorpat, creating a continuous main line of resistance. As a result, beyond Lake Wirtz the XXXXIII Army Corps was again in direct contact with positions of the III SS Panzer Corps. The Wehrmacht communiqué of 22 August 1944 declared:

"*West of Lake Pskov, a battle group from the SS Assault Brigade 'Wallonien' under the command of SS-Sturmbannführer Degrelle distinguished itself through its tenacity and offensive élan.*"

Two days later, however, the Red Army was able to occupy Dorpat and establish a bridgehead over the Embach. They then initially halted their offensive in this area, not least because of their heavy losses.

The Wallonian SS battle group, which had sustained very heavy losses in killed and wounded in the fierce fighting near Noela (northwest of Dorpat) and at the Soviet bridgehead, received 200 replacements from Debica at the end of August 1944. In mid-September, during the course of the general retreat, the men were ordered out of Estonia and back to Debica for the formation of the SS Volunteer Grenadier Division "*Wallonien*".

The 28th SS Volunteer Grenadier Division "*Wallonien*" (Wallonian No. 1)

As he had done with the Flemings, on 18 September 1944 Himmler used the vast number of "*volunteers*" as justification for the formation of the 28th SS Volunteer Grenadier Division "*Wallonien*". Here, too, in reality the numbers were quite different. Nevertheless, the 28th SS Volunteer Grenadier Division "*Wallonien*" was supposed to have the following organization:

SS Volunteer Grenadier Regiment 69 (Wallonian No. 1) (2 battalions)	SS-Hauptsturmführer Mathieu
SS Volunteer Grenadier Regiment 70 (Wallonian No. 2) (2 battalions)	SS-Sturmbannführer Tchekhoff
SS Volunteer Grenadier Regiment 71	(not formed)
SS-Division Fusilier Battalion 28	(not formed)
SS Anti-Tank Battalion 28	
1st Company (75-mm Pak 40)	SS-Obersturmführer Lamproye
2nd Company (20-mm Flak 38)	SS-Obersturmführer Thyssen
SS Volunteer Artillery Regiment 28	SS-Hauptsturmführer Malherbe
SS Pioneer Battalion 28	SS-Obersturmführer Wirgain
SS Signals Battalion 28	SS-Hauptsturmführer Schmitt
SS Supply Company 28	SS-Untersturmführer Jacobs
SS Administration Company 28	SS-Untersturmführer Plaumann
SS Medical Company 28	SS-Obersturmführer Stahl
SS Veterinary Company 28	SS-Hauptsturmführer Dr. Quast

SS Operational Headquarters had selected *SS-Oberführer* Burk to be division commander, but when the time came for the formation order to be issued, just 1,500 soldiers were on hand, and it was clear that the unit would never come close to its authorized strength. *SS-Sturmbannführer* Degrelle, former commander of the 5th SS Volunteer Assault Brigade, was instead named division leader. Interestingly, he signed his name as "*division commander*" (*Divisionskommandeur*) and not "division leader" (*Divisionsführer*) as befitted his rank.

The large-scale recruitment campaign of 1943-44 had only attracted a few hundred recruits in Belgium, and now the primary source of volunteers was the approximately 15,000 Wallonian collaborators evacuated to Germany.[38]

[38] Belgium was occupied by Allied troops on 3 September 1944.

The SS Volunteer Brigade "*Wallonien*" during training in Wildflecken.

75-mm Pak 40 anti-tank gun.

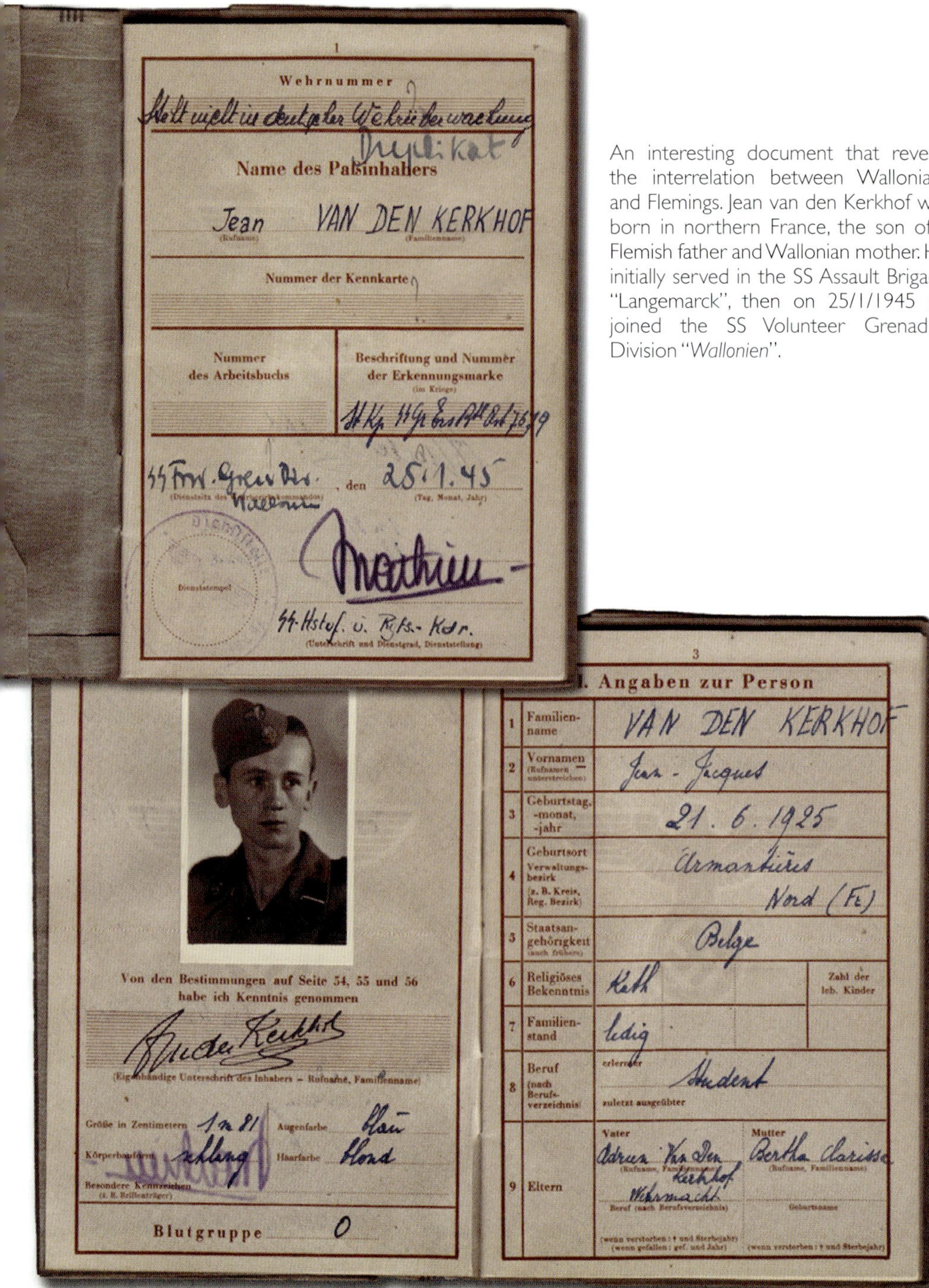

An interesting document that reveals the interrelation between Wallonians and Flemings. Jean van den Kerkhof was born in northern France, the son of a Flemish father and Wallonian mother. He initially served in the SS Assault Brigade "Langemarck", then on 25/1/1945 he joined the SS Volunteer Grenadier Division "*Wallonien*".

The unit's actual strength on 30 September 1944 was:

	Officers	NCOs	Enlisted Men	Total
Actual	70	265	1,230	1,565
	4.47%	16.93%	78.60%	100%
Authorized	443	2,262	9,926	12,621
	3.4%	17.9%	78.7%	100%

SS-Sturmbannführer Degrelle, at least, realized that 11,000 more Wallonian were not going to volunteer to serve in the division; consequently, he proposed that the French militia and Spanish volunteers in Wildflecken be integrated into his unit. This was a not uninteresting idea, for in this way uncommitted formations could be concentrated in a large formation for frontline use. Moreover, about 100 Frenchmen (former armaments workers) had already served in the 5th SS Volunteer Assault Brigade. Not least because of political reservations about a merging of French and Wallonian soldiers, only the Spanish SS company (remnants of the Spanish Legion) were attached to the 28th SS Volunteer Grenadier Division "*Wallonien*".

A transfer order into the Gronau area (south of Hanover) was issued on 18 October 1944. SS Operational Headquarters issued a completely unrealistic order for the division to achieve operational readiness by 31 March 1945. It expected a division to be formed in just under six months, even though it presently had just 12% of its authorized strength.

On 20 December 1944, during the German "Rundstedt offensive" (Ardennes offensive), SS Volunteer Grenadier Regiment 69 and its two battalions were ordered into the Cologne – Rommerskirchen – Liblar – Bliesheim – Lechenich – Rheydt area. As the division had been formed solely for use on the Eastern Front in the war against Bolshevism, the regiment's main purpose was to simulate German forces for the benefit of Allied intelligence. Whereas the Flemish SS Battle Group "*Schellong*", which had also been sent to the Commander-in-Chief West, remained in old Reich territory, the Wallonian SS Battle Group "Mathieu" was briefly moved into the Limerlé area (approx. 25 km southwest of St. Vith).

When the Ardennes offensive was halted, both battalions were ordered back into the Gronau area. There, on 19 January 1945, orders arrived for the unit to be reorganized as an Infantry Division 1945, which had a lower authorized strength. The only change brought about by this order was that instead of being approximately 8,000 men short, the division was now only about 5,000 men below authorized strength. Actual strength at that time was on the order of about 3,000 men.

On 30 January 1945 the unit received orders to form a regiment-strength battle group and move it to the Stargard area in preparation for the planned offensive in Pomerania. The two battalions of SS Volunteer Grenadier Regiment 69 plus I

Battalion, SS Volunteer Grenadier Regiment 70 were sent by rail to the XXXIX Panzer Corps (11th Army). The three battalions initially occupied positions in the Kremzow – Repplin area along the Faulen Ihna, protecting Stargard, an important railway junction, against advancing enemy forces. A bridgehead position was captured near Krüssow to secure added jumping-off positions for the coming offensive.

When the German offensive began on 16 February 1945, the no longer motorized Wallonian battle group attacked over the Linden Hills toward Muscherin on the right wing of the 10th SS Panzer Division "*Frundsberg*". Contrary to expectations, the units were able to gain little ground, and already on 17-18 February were forced onto the defensive. During the fighting, the 7th Company of SS Volunteer Grenadier Regiment 69 under *SS-Obersturmführer* Capelle held its positions in the Linden Hills to the last man. Of the company's personnel 61 were wounded. The rest, including the company commander, were killed. The entire Pomeranian offensive was called off after a few days and the troops were pulled back beyond the Ihna. For the Walloons, this meant a withdrawal toward the Collin – Strebelow area and Kremzow.

After the XXXIX Panzer Corps (including the 10th SS Panzer Division "*Frundsberg*") was withdrawn from the area on 23 February 1945, the Wallonian SS battle group and the 11th SS Volunteer Panzer Grenadier Division "*Nordland*" were attached to the newly-formed Panzer Corps Group[39] Munzel.

The *Wehrmacht* communiqué of 27 February 1945 reported the selfless sacrifice of the 7th Company, SS Volunteer Grenadier Regiment 69 on 17 February:

"*In Pomerania, a battle group of the SS Volunteer Grenadier Division 'Wallonien' under the command of SS-Obersturmführer Capelle assigned to provide flanking cover battled with exemplary steadfastness and fanatical determination.*"

On 1 March 1945 the Soviets launched their own offensive in Pomerania, and within a few hours brought the German front to collapse. On 3 March the Wallonian SS volunteers were forced to begin withdrawing toward Stargard. On 6 March the survivors withdrew from the line Streesen (SS Volunteer Grenadier Regiment 69) – Schöneberg (I Battalion, SS Volunteer Grenadier Regiment 70) through Lübow (approx. 5 km northeast of Stargard) to Bruchhausen (approx. 10 km northwest of Stargard). The next day the completely exhausted men reached Altdamm by way of Münsterberg and Augustenwalde (approx. 12 km east of Stettin). There the front calmed down, at least briefly.

SS-Obersturmbannführer Degrelle and the remnants of his unit marched to Scheune (west of Stettin) where, attached to the XXXII Army Corps, it was given

[39] The (Division) Group "Munzel" had originally been formed from various alert units; now its staff assumed the functions of a corps headquarters. See the Army Group Vistula situation map.

a week's rest. When Degrelle gave the survivors the option of leaving the fighting forces, about 80 Walloons took advantage of the opportunity. A new, smaller battle group was formed from the remnants of the former one, and on 16 March 1945 it moved into the Altdamm bridgehead in front of Finkenwalde with 23 officers and 650 other ranks.

On 9 March 1945 while the battalion, which was ultimately designated I Battalion, SS Volunteer Grenadier Regiment 69 was in costly action near Altdamm, SS Operational Headquarters ordered the formation of another battle group for action on the Oder Front. Whereas in the previous weeks the men had had nothing more than panzerfausts to use against the enemy's massed tank attacks, in hard fought-over Finkenwalde the Walloons had some support, including two Panzer IVs.

After it had become clear that an attack from there was no longer possible, on 20 March 1945 Hitler authorized the evacuation of the bridgehead. About 200 Walloons pulled back across the Oder. This ended the fighting in the Stettin area for about four weeks. About 450 men had been killed or wounded in just four days of fighting!

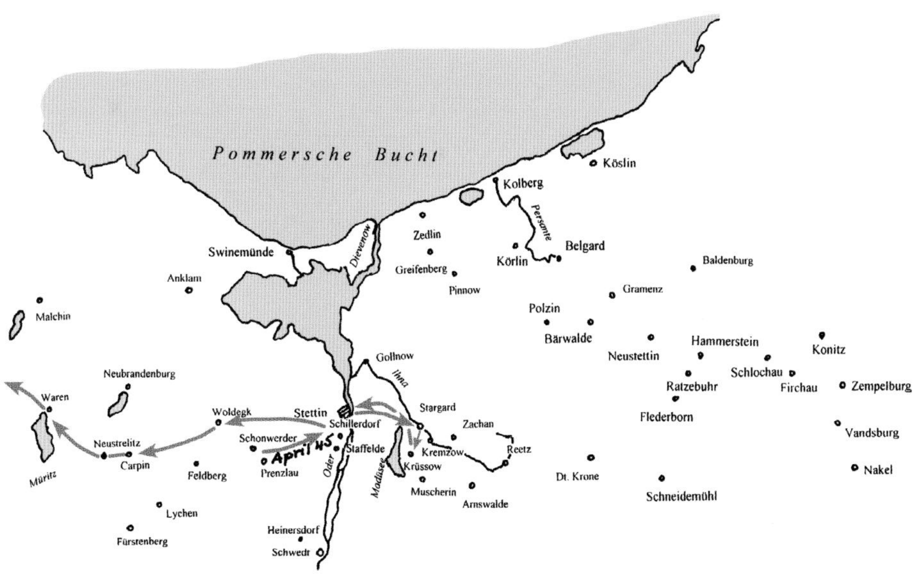

Karte: Der Einsatz in Pommern und Mecklenburg (Februar bis Mai 1945).

Map: Actions in Pomerania and Mecklenburg (February to May 1945).

On 26 March 1945 *General der Panzertruppen* von Manteuffel, Commander-in-Chief of the 3rd Panzer Army, assessed the Wallonian SS unit:

"The division is no more than a regiment group, presently consisting of an operational strength battalion with another of medium strength in formation. The soldiers are less steady than the members of 'Langemarck' and after setbacks require a period of rest and refurbishment. Little concern for weapons, battle group not suitable for offensive tasks, only for defense."

While the remains of I Battalion, SS Volunteer Grenadier Regiment 69 were resting in the Stettin area, *SS-Obersturmbannführer* Degrelle drove to Gronau to oversee the formation of the second battle group. The approximately 900 artillerymen and pioneers sent to the Protectorate of Bohemia and Moravia for training had meanwhile returned there. A short time earlier, 200 recruits from Gronau had been mobilized by the Wehrmacht and were armed with panzerfausts in order to halt an advance by American armor near Holzminden. As the Walloons were supposed to be used exclusively against the Red Army, Degrelle intervened and obtained their release. Conscious of the agony of the German Reich, he subsequently also demobilized the Wallonian convalescents staying in the Gronau barracks.

Although SS Operational Headquarters had ordered the formation of a battle group equal in strength to a grenadier regiment plus an anti-tank battalion, Degrelle only formed a battalion with about 950 men. Its equipment included:

35 light machine-guns
2 motorcycles
3 automobiles
1 truck
256 horses

The men were transported by rail to the so-called Oder Corps, part of the 3rd Panzer Army, arriving in the area south of Stettin on 6 April 1945. There Degrelle gave approximately 200 men the opportunity to leave the combat units, and from those who remained he reformed the II Battalion, SS Volunteer Grenadier Regiment 69.

On 13 April 1945 the high command of Army Group Vistula issued the following order:

"In keeping with the wishes of the Reichsführer-SS, the following units are operationally attached to the III (Germanic) SS Panzer Corps:

SS Volunteer Brigade 'Wallonien'
SS Volunteer Brigade 'Charlemagne'
Rumanian SS-Regiment
Tactical attachment of the SS Volunteer Brigade 'Wallonien' not possible, as it is intervention reserve in the Stettin area."

Because of the situation, it was not possible to bring together the various small SS battle groups under the high command of the III (Germanic) SS Panzer Corps, whose headquarters were in Templin. Instead, two days later a mixed Belgian division group was formed under *SS-Standartenführer* Müller, commander of the 27th SS Volunteer Grenadier Division "*Langemarck*". Attached to the Oder Corps, it represented an intervention reserve in the Hohenholz area (east of the Randow Valley).

On 19 April 1945 the 3rd Panzer Army was organized as follows:

XXXII Army Corps with
- Oberst Ledebur Group
- 549th Volks-Grenadier Division
- Fortress Stettin
- 281st Infantry Division

Oder Corps with
- Special Purpose Division 610
- I Battalion, SS Volunteer Grenadier Regiment 66 (Flemish No. 1)
- I Battalion, SS Volunteer Artillery Regiment 27 (Flemish No. 1)
- SS Volunteer Grenadier Regiment 69 (Wallonian No. 1)
- Assault Battalion, 3rd Panzer Army
- Anti-Tank Battalion 6

XXXXVI Panzer Corps with
- 547th Volks-Grenadier Division
- Artillery Commander 406
- 1st Marine Division

On 20 April 1945 the Red Army succeeded in crossing the Oder south of Stettin near Wilhelmshöhe and established a bridgehead there. In response, SS Battle Group Hellebaut was formed from:

I Battalion, SS Volunteer Grenadier Regiment 66
I Battalion, SS Volunteer Grenadier Regiment 69
Anti-Tank Battalion 6
Assault Battalion, 3rd Panzer Army

In the subsequent heavy fighting the battle group was unable to seal off the penetrations, however. The next day enemy advances forced the men to withdraw toward the II Battalion, SS Volunteer Grenadier Regiment 69's line of security near Staffelde.

After the high command of the Oder Corps commanded by *SS-Obergruppenführer* von dem Bach proved incapable of directing large-scale combat operations, on 23 April 1945 the staffs were exchanged. The high command of the XXXXVI Panzer Corps now commanded in the area of the former Oder Corps high command and vice versa. But even the new command could not prevent the Red Army from breaching the so-called Wotan Position along the Randow Valley on 25-26 April 1945. The Walloons withdrew west through Brüssow. The Commander-in-Chief of the 3rd Panzer Army, *General der Panzertruppen* von Manteuffel, described the situation on 27 April 1945 very graphically:

"*Complete disintegration of the units 'Langemarck', 'Wallonien', 1st Marine Division and all of the flak battalions, insofar as they lost their weapons through their own fault or not. I didn't witness such scenes as this even in 1918.*"

After the so-called Uecker position and the "Wotan Position" were immediately breached, the same day Manteuffel ordered the occupation of the so-called Feldberg position. There he intended to restore order to the defense. SS Battle Group Hellebaut pulled back via Schönwerder and Holzendorf to Woldegk. Near Carpin it encountered approximately 500 members of the 33rd SS Waffen Grenadier Division "*Charlemagne*" and marched with them to Neustrelitz. They reached Waren, together with civilians, Wehrmacht elements, and concentration camp inmates (satellite camp of the Sachsenhausen concentration camp).

On 30 April 1945 *SS-Obersturmbannführer* Degrelle and *SS-Standartenführer* Müller met in Nossentiner Hütte. Together they wanted to try to get their units to Lübeck. At the very worst they wanted to be taken prisoner by the western Allies. From Lübeck the Wallonian and Flemish volunteers were to occupy quarters in the Bad Segeberg area. Orders were overtaken by the Allied advance and Lübeck and Bad Segeberg were occupied almost without a fight. Beginning on 2 May 1945, the bulk of the remaining members of the 28th SS Volunteer Grenadier Division "*Wallonien*" marched into captivity.

First assembled in the camp at Fallingbostel, the Walloons were returned to Belgium in several transports by the end of 1946 and handed over to the Belgian authorities. Mass trials began in 1947, and most Eastern Front volunteers were at least given prison sentences and deprived of their civil rights for several years. Rutja Delanoye recalled his time in the *Waffen-SS*:

"I was born in Westende on 23 December 1927 and falsified my birth date to 1924 so that I would be accepted as a volunteer in the Legion Wallonie. I was called up on 28 March 1943 at the age of 16 and reported to Meseritz. At the end of June I arrived at Training Camp Wildflecken. As part of the 5th SS Volunteer Assault Brigade 'Wallonien', I took part in the fighting in the Cherkassy Pocket until I was wounded on 7 February 1944. I was taken via Uman to a Luftwaffe hospital in Glatz and on 1 April 1944 I was given four weeks leave. At the end of April 1944 I left Brussels again for SS Training Camp Heidelager, where I was presented with the Assault Badge and the Wound Badge in Black. I was also promoted to SS-Sturmmann. From 16 July 1944 I was a member of SS Battle Group 'Wallonien', which saw action in the Dorpat area in Estonia. I was wounded again on 18 August 1944 and was taken to a hospital in Reval. There I was awarded the Iron Cross, Second Class. Four weeks later we were evacuated to Danzig by ship and I was assigned to our replacement unit in Breslau (SS Grenadier Training and Replacement Battalion 360). This was followed by a transfer to the Western Front in December 1944 and action in Pomerania in spring 1945. After the heavy fighting in the Altdamm bridgehead and later south of Stettin, on 13 May 1945 I was captured by the Americans. They handed me over to the English ten days later, and on 24 October 1945 they in turn handed me over to the Belgian authorities."

129

28.SS-Freiw.Gren.Division "Wallonien"
Ia. Tgb. Nr. 129/45

Gef.Std., den 14.3.1945.

G.Kdos. 5 Ausfertigungen
3. Ausfertigung

H

Betr.: Aufstellung der Kampfgruppe "Wallonien"

An das
III.Germ.SS-Pz.Korps.

Bericht über die Umgruppierung der 28.SS-Freiw.Gren.Div."Wallonien"

Vor ihrer vollkommenen Aufstellung waren die beiden Btl. des 69.SS-Rgts. seit dem 20.Dezember 1944 im Westen und seit dem 6.2.1945 im Raume südl. Stargard eingesetzt. Sie waren in den letzten Tagen an folgenden Gefechten im Raume von Stargard beteiligt:

1). Angriff und Einbringung von Gefangenen bei Karlsburg — am 1.3.45
2) Verteidigung der Höhe 43 (ostwärts Krüssow) — am 1.3.45
3) Sicherung der Absetzbewegung des 23.SS-Rgts."Norge" bei Blomberg und Kollin — am 2.3.45
4) Verteidigung des Südteils des Ortes Kremsow — am 2.3.45
5) Sicherung der Absetzbewegung des III./23.SS-Rgt. "Norge" bei Schneidersfelde — am 3.3.45
6) Verteidigung von Schneidersfelde, Strebelow, Krüssow — am 3.3.45
7) Deckung der Absetzbewegungen der 281.I.D. bei Streesen, Wittichow und Verteidigung der Ihna, südlich Stargard bis 23.00 Uhr. — am 4.3.45
8) Äusserst schwierige Absetzbewegung über Klützow, Moritzfelde bis Seefeld in der Nacht vom 4/5.3.45. Diese Absetzbewegung wurde allein durch die Sicherung einer Kampfgruppe des 70.SS-Rgts."Wallonien", die am Westrande von Stargard heftig angegriffen wurde, ermöglicht.
9) Verteidigung von Lübow, Saarow, Bruchhausen im Laufe des 6.3.45 gegen eine grössere Anzahl Panzer mit aufgesessener Infanterie.
10) Absetzbewegungen über Münsterberg, Augustwalde bis Altdamm und Stettin in der Nacht vom 6/7.3.45.

Im Verlaufe dieser Gefechte und Absetzbewegungen hat die kämpfende Truppe, die nur über einen unzureichenden und oft improvisierten bespannten Tross verfügte, einen grossen Teil ihrer Waffen und Ausrüstung verloren. Der Anschluss inerhalb der Trosse war zum grossen Teil nicht vorhanden, da sich auf der Strasse über Moritzfelde in Richtung auf Altdamm und die Oder Trosse mehrerer Einheiten und zahlreiche Evakuierte der Gegend Stargard mit ihren Fahrzeugen in grosser Unordnung bewegten.
Dem deutschen Soldaten ist es leicht Auskunft über den Aufenthaltsort seiner Einheit und über seinen Auftrag zu erhalten. Der wallonische Soldat jedoch verirrt sich viel leichter und fühlt sich in schwierigen Situationen schnell abgeschnitten.
Unter diesen Umständen war es nicht möglich die Einheit früher als am 8. März in Scheune zu sammeln, sie zu verpflegen und der Truppe etwas Ruhe zu gewähren. Die Mehrzahl der Männer hatte seit 5-6 Tagen nicht geschlafen und kämpfend 80 Km. zurückgelegt.
Die uns zur Verfügung stehenden Waffen und Fahrzeuge haben es erlaubt nun eine Kampfgruppe zusammenzustellen, die aus dem besten infanteristischen Menschenmaterial der beiden Btl. besteht.
In der Anlage eine Gliederung dieser Kampfgruppe.
Im Augenblick ist es nicht möglich noch andere Kampfeinheiten aufzustellen. Im Verlaufe der letzten Gefechte sind mehrere Hundert gefallen oder vermisst, sowie verwundet worden. Mehrere Hundert, die entweder zu jung oder zu alt sind und die im Augenblick des Ein-

satzes weder über genug Erfahrung noch Ausbildung verfügten, sind sowohl physisch wie moralisch noch zu erschöpft um sofort eingesetzt zu werden.

Im Sinne des Befehls vom SS-FHA., Amt II/Org.Ia vom 9.März 45, schlage ich vor, diese zum Einsatz untaugliche Teile in Begleitung des Rahmenpersonals für die Ausbildung der neuaufzustellenden Einheiten der Division sowie der zum Kampfeinsatz unnötigen Teile der Division (Nachr.Kp., San.Kp., Vet.Kp., Feldzeug-Kp., I-Zug) in den Raum um Hannover zu leiten, wie bereits beschlossen.

Für das Divisionskommando
Der 1.Generalstabsoffizier
A.B.

SS-Sturmbannführer.

K a m p f g r u p p e

28.SS-Freiw.Gren.Division "Wallonien"

15-3.45

a) Divisionskommando (gekürzt)

Kommandeur:	SS-Obersturmbannführer	Léon Degrelle
Ia. :	SS-Sturmbannführer	Hellebaut
Ord.-Off. :	SS-Untersturmführer	Forster
:	SS-Untersturmführer	Gombert

3 Schreiber (Unterführer)
3 Kfz.-Fahrer
3 Kradmelder

b) Kampfgruppe-Stab

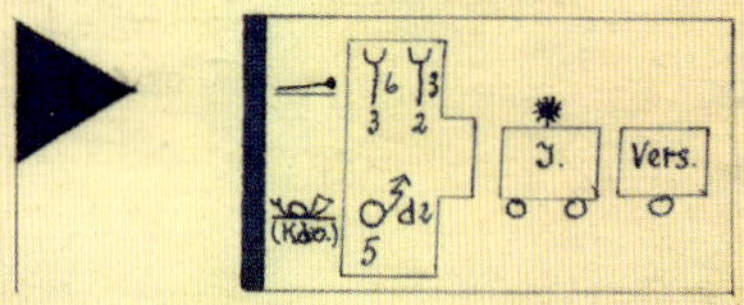

Btl-Kommandeur :	SS-Hauptsturmführer	Derrikx
Adjutant :	SS-Untersturmführer	Sandron
Ord.-Off. :	SS-Untersturmführer	De Goy
:	SS-Untersturmführer	Gillemon
Arzt (IVb) :	SS-Obersturmführer	Buy
IVa :	SS-Untersturmführer	Zepletal
TFK :	SS-Untersturmführer	Ducaté

c) Grenadier-Bataillon

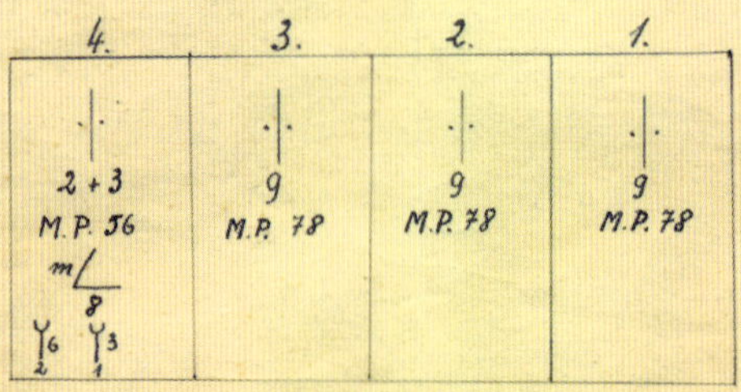

28. SS-Freiw. Gren. Division **Geheim**
"Wallonien".

Kommandeur.
Tgb. Nr. II/488/45 Geh.

O. U., den 14. März 1945. W

Betr.: Transportgenehmigung von Restteilen der Division für die vom SS-Führungshauptamt genehmigte Neuaufstellung von Div. Einheiten im Raum Elze (Hann.).-

An:

Heeres-Gruppe Weichsel.

Durch FS vom 9.3.45. SS-Führungshauptamt, Amt II/Org. Abt. Ia/II wurde der Division Aufstellung von folgenden Einheiten befohlen:

Wortlaut der Abschrift des FS v. 9.3.45.

"An 28. SS-Freiw. Gren. Division "Wallonien".

Bezug: SS-FHA Amt II Org. Abt. Ia/II Tgb. No. 3712/44 geh. vom 19.10.44., SS-FHA Amt II Org. Abt. Ia Tgb. No. II/20740/44 geh. vom 11.12.44.-

1) Im Rahmen der Aufstellung der 28. SS-Freiw. Gren. Division "Wallonien" sind aus dem noch zur Verfügung stehenden wallonischen Personal im Raum um Gronau (W. Kdo. XI) vorerst folgende Div. Einheiten aufzustellen und nach Fertigstellung der bei HGruppe Weichsel im Einsatz befindlichen Div. Kampfgruppe Wallonien zuzuführen:

1 Gren. Regiment,
1 Pz. Jäger Abtlg.,
1 gem. Na. Kp. (ohne 1 Zug)
nach KStN 4075 vom 1.2.44.,
2 Fahrschwadronen (30 to) ohne im Einsatz befindl. Teile
Kfz. Instands. Zug -"- -"-
Veterinär Kp. -"- -"-
San. Kp. m. Krkw. Zug -"- -"-

Gliederung und mot. Bestimmung gelten gem. Verfg. SS-FHA Amt II Org. Abt. Ia/II Tgb. No. 3712/44 gKdos. vom 19.10.44.-

2) Zur verantwortlichen Durchführung der Aufstellung ist durch die Division ein kleiner Aufstellungsstab in den Raum Gronau abzustellen. Der Aufstellungsstab untersteht mit den aufzustellenden Div. Einheiten bis auf Weiteres dem SS-FHA In. 2 unmittelbar.

3) Heeresgruppe Weichsel wird gebeten, die für den derzeitigen Einsatz der Div. Kampfgruppe Wallonien nicht benötigten Pers. und mot. Teile in den Aufstellungsraum der Div. nach Gronau zuzuführen.-

4) W.Kdo. XI wird gebeten, im Raum um Gronau Unterbringungsmöglichkeiten für 3500 Mann sicherzustellen. Führer des Aufstellungsstabes nimmt hierzu mit W.Kdo. XI Verbindung auf.-

5) Durchgeführte Aufstellung der Div. Einheiten, sowie Inmarsch - setzung zur Div. Kampfgruppe "Wallonien" istdem SS-FHA Org. Abt. I a zu melden.-

SS-FHA Amt II/Org. Abt. Ia/II,
gez. Blume, SS-Obstubaf.

Die Division wurde am 7.3.45. auf Befehl des SS-Pz. A.K. III im Raum ostwärts Stettin herausgelöst.-

-2-

-2-

Mit dem Auftrag, nach einer Versammlungs- und Ruhezeit von 6 - 8 Tagen, durch Bildung einer Kampfgruppe, wieder eingesetzt zu werden.-

Aus den vorhandenen ausgebildeten Führern, Unterführern und Mannschaften wird zurzeit eine Kampfgruppe in Stärke von 700 - 800 Mann gebildet.-

Die in der Division noch vorhandenen Waffen und materielle Ausrüstung, sowie Pferde mit entspr. Mot.-Teilen, werden dazu benötigt.-

Der Restteil an Mannschaften, ausser Stämmen, Versorgungs-Truppen in Stärke von ca. 450 Führern, Unterführern und Mannschaften, sind für die befohlene Neuaufstellung erforderlich.-

Es wird gebeten, die Überführung der Restteile raschmöglichst durchführen zu dürfen, da für diese Teile keine Waffen vorhanden sind, nur mangelhafte Bekleidung, und keine ausreichende Versorgungsmöglichkeit in diesem Raum besteht (Mangel an Feldküchen und völlige Unbeweglichkeit).-

Durch Vorstehendes, dazu noch die Unterbringungsschwierigkeiten ist eine Ausbildung und Aufstellung in diesem Raum nicht möglich. Es wird gebeten, entsprechende Befehle erteilen zu wollen.-

ϟϟ-Obersturmbannführer und
Divisions - Kommandeur.

Oberkommando der Heeresgruppe Weichsel   H.Qu., 15. März 1945
Ia/Nr. 2952/45 geh.Kdos.

Geheime Kommandosache!
6 Ausfertigungen
6. Ausfertigung

Bezug: 1.) 28.SS-Freiw.Gren.Div."Wallonien" / Ia/Nr.129/45 g.K. v.14.3.45 an III.Germ.SS-Pz.Korps.

2.) 28.SS-Freiw.Gren.Div."Wallonien" Nr.II/488/45 geh.v. 14.3.45.

An
Pz. A.O.K. 3

Die für Führung und Versorgung der Kampfgruppe "Wallonien" nicht benötigten Teile (Nachr.Kp., San-Kp., Vetr.Kp., sowie überzähliges Gerät) sind zur Verfügung des SS - F H A im E-Transport nach Gronau (W.Kr. XI) zur Aufstellung der 2. Kampfgruppe der SS-Gren. Div. "Wallonien" zuzuführen. Feldzeugkp. und J-Zug sind bis zum Eintreffen des Versorgungs-Regts. 193 der 1. Marine - Div. taktisch zu unterstellen und anschliessend nach Gronau in Marsch zu setzen. Die z.Zt. infolge fehlender Bewaffnung und Ausrüstung nicht einsatzfähigen Teile der Div. "Wallonien" (300 - 400 Mann) sind im frontnahen Raum aufzufrischen und zu einem weiteren Batl. für Kampfgruppe "Wallonien" neu aufzustellen. Fehlendes Material ist bei SS - F H A anzufordern.

Für das Oberkommando der Heeresgruppe Weichsel
Der Chef des Generalstabes

Nachr.:
2. O Qu
3. Gen.d.Tra.
4. Obersturmbannführer Grothmann
5. Sturmbannführer Hallwachs.
6. Id (E)

Appendix

Division Commanders

5th SS Panzer Division "*Wiking*"

12/40 – 10/42 *SS-Obergruppenführer* Steiner

Felix Steiner was born in Stallupönen on 23 May 1896, and in March 1914 joined the 5th Infantry Regiment "von Boyen" No. 41 in Tilsit as an officer candidate. On 27 January 1915 he received his *Leutnant*'s commission. After serving first on the Eastern Front and then on the Western Front, Steiner was promoted to *Oberleutnant* on 10 October 1918. After demobilization he joined the *Freikorps*, and in 1921 the *Reichswehr*. On 1 December 1927 he was promoted to *Hauptmann*. Discharged in 1933, he came to the *SS-Verfügungstruppe* (armed SS) by way of the Chef AW (SA training section). As an *SS-Obersturmbannführer* he became commander of III Battalion, *SS Standarte 1* in Ellwangen and later, following promotion to *SS-Standartenführer* on 1 July 1936, the *SS Standarte "Deutschland"*. After seeing action in Poland, on 15 August 1940 Steiner was awarded the Knight's Cross of the Iron Cross for his actions during the Western Campaign. Promoted to *SS-Brigadeführer* on 9 November 1940, in December 1940 he was tasked with the formation of the SS-Division "*Wiking*". On 30 January 1942 he was promoted to the rank of *SS-Gruppenführer*, and on 23 December 1942 was awarded the Knight's Cross with Oak Leaves. In May 1943 Hitler named him commanding general of the newly-formed III (Germanic) SS Panzer Corps. During the course of this Steiner was promoted to *SS-Obergruppenführer und General der Waffen-SS*. In recognition of the corps' success, on 10 August 1944 he was awarded the Knight's Cross with Oak Leaves and Swords. In late October 1944 Steiner fell ill with jaundice. After his recovery, in late January 1945 he served briefly as Commander-in-Chief of the 11th Army in Pomerania. At the end of March 1945 he took charge of assembling the scattered *Wehrmacht* and *Waffen-SS* units west of the Oder and was finally placed in command of Army Group Steiner, which was supposed to relieve Berlin from the north. As this mission could not be accomplished under the existing circumstances, Steiner refused the order and consequently was relieved of his post by Hitler on 27 April 1945. On 3 May 1945 he was captured by the Americans at the Elbe and was held until 27 April 1948. Steiner was charged with war crimes, however, these were subsequently dropped. He later wrote a number of books, including *Die Armee der Geächteten*. Steiner died in Munich on 12 May 1966.

10/42 – 08/44 *SS-Obergruppenführer* Gille

Herbert Gille was born in Gandersheim on 8 March 1897, and in 1910 he joined the Royal Prussian Cadet Corps. He served in the First World War, initially in Field Artillery Regiment 55 and later Field Artillery Regiment 30. Wounded several times, he was demobilized in 1919 with the rank of *Oberleutnant*. He worked as an estate manager until 1934 and then joined the *SS-Verfügungstruppe*. By 1937 he had achieved the rank of *SS-Sturmbannführer*. After completing a course for battalion commanders at the infantry school in Döberitz, in 1938 Gille assumed command of II Battalion, *SS Standarte "Der Führer"*. When the SS Artillery *Standarte* (*SS-Verfügungstruppe*) was formed he was named commander of its I Battalion. On 15 November 1940 Gille was named commander of SS Artillery Regiment 5, and on 30 January 1941 was promoted to *SS-Standartenführer*. Promotion to the rank of *SS-Oberführer* followed on 1 October 1941, and one week later he was awarded the Knight's Cross for his success in leading elements of the SS-Division "*Wiking*". Gille was promoted to *SS-Brigadeführer* on 1 December 1942, and on 1 May 1943 he assumed command of the Panzer Grenadier Division "*Wiking*". On 1 November 1943 he was awarded the Knight's Cross with Oak Leaves, and one week later was promoted to *SS-Gruppenführer*. For his command of the division in the Cherkassy Pocket, Gille was awarded the Knight's Cross with Oak Leaves and Swords on 20 February 1944. Soon afterward Gille directed the defense of Kovel, a vital rail junction, for which he was awarded the Knight's Cross with Oak Leaves, Swords and Diamonds on 19 April 1944. In August 1944 he was named commanding general of the IV SS Panzer Corps, and on 9 November was promoted to *SS-Obergruppenführer*. When the war ended Gille was taken prisoner by the Americans and was subsequently released in 1948. He was charged with no war crimes. After the war he founded "*Wiking Ruf*", a magazine for former members of the *Waffen-SS*. Gille died in Stemmen on 27 December 1966.

08/44 – 10/44 *SS-Standartenführer* Mühlenkamp

Johannes Mühlenkamp was born in Montigny-lès-Metz on 9 October 1910, and in September 1934 he joined the *SS Standarte "Germania"*. After passing through the *SS Junkerschule "Braunschweig"*, on 20 April 1936 he was promoted to *SS-Untersturmführer*. After promotion to the rank of *SS-Obersturmführer*, in 1938 he assumed command of the 15th Company, *SS Standarte "Germania"*. From June to November 1940 Mühlenkamp served in the staff of the *SS-Verfügungstruppe* as IIa (division adjutant). He was promoted to *SS-Hauptsturmführer* on 9 November 1940. He subsequently assumed command of the SS Reconnaissance Battalion "*Reich*". Mühlenkamp was awarded the German Cross in Gold on 2 January 1942, and on 30 January was promoted to *SS-Sturmbannführer*. In June he was given command of SS Panzer Battalion 5 of the SS-Division "*Wiking*", and on 3 September 1941 he was awarded the Knight's Cross of the Iron Cross. Promoted to *SS-Obersturmbannführer* on 30 January 1943, in March 1944 Mühlenkamp assumed command of SS Panzer Regiment 5. Following promotion to *SS-Standartenführer* on 20 April 1944, on 6 August he was temporarily placed in command of the 5th SS Panzer Division "*Wiking*". He was awarded the Knight's Cross with Oak Leaves on 21 September 1944. In October 1944 he became Inspector of *Waffen-SS* Armored Forces in SS Operational Headquarters. Then, in February 1945, he was briefly placed in command of the newly-formed 32nd SS Volunteer Grenadier Division "30 January" on the Oder Front. He was wounded there, ending his wartime service. Mühlenkamp died in Goslar on 23 September 1986.

10/44 – 05/45 *SS-Oberführer* Ullrich

Karl Ullrich was born in Saargemünd on 1 December 1910, and from 1 June 1933 he served briefly in Infantry Regiment 19. He subsequently transferred to the police service, and on 1 July 1934 joined the 1st Company of the *SS Standarte*. In March 1935 he was sent to the *SS Junkerschule "Braunschweig"* for officer training, and after graduating on 25 February 1936 he was given the rank of *SS-Standartenoberjunker*. Ullrich was promoted to *SS-Untersturmführer* on 1 April 1936 and *SS-Obersturmführer* on 1 September 1937. He took part in the campaigns against Poland and in the west as an *SS-Hauptsturmführer* and commander of 3rd Company, SS Pioneer Sturmbann. Ullrich was given command of the SS Pioneer Battalion "*Totenkopf*" in the spring of 1941. After promotion to *SS-Sturmbannführer* on 1 November 1941, on 19 February 1942 he was awarded the Knight's Cross. He became commander of III Battalion, *SS Totenkopf Panzer Grenadier Regiment 1* in March 1943. Then, on 10 September 1943 he was placed in command of SS Panzer Grenadier Regiment 6. Ullrich was promoted to *SS-Obersturmbannführer* on 9 November 1943, and on 14 May 1944 was awarded the Knight's Cross with Oak Leaves. Six weeks later he was promoted to *SS-Standartenführer*, and on 9 October 1944 was placed in command of the 5th SS Panzer Division "*Wiking*". He was subsequently promoted to *SS-Oberführer*, and on 12 May 1945 was captured by the Americans. Ullrich was released in September 1948. He died in Bad Reichenhall on 8 May 1996.

27th SS Volunteer Grenadier Division "*Langemarck*"

12/44 – 05/45 *SS-Standartenführer* Müller

Thomas Müller was born in Munich on 2 February 1902. After joining the SS, by 11 September 1934 he achieved the rank of *SS-Untersturmführer*. He subsequently commanded the 4th Company, *SS Standarte "Deutschland"* from 1 June 1936 to 16 September 1938, first as an *SS-Obersturmführer* and, from 9 November 1936, as an *SS-Hauptsturmführer*. On 1 November 1939 he was given command of I Battalion, *SS Standarte "Der Führer"*, which he led until 1 February 1941. Following promotion to *SS-Sturmbannführer* and, on 20 April 1942, to *SS-Obersturmbannführer*, on 1 February 1943 Müller was appointed commander of the SS school for non-commissioned officers in Radolfszell. When the SS Panzer Grenadier Division "*Hohenstaufen*" was formed, he was given command of SS Panzer Grenadier Regiment 20. Müller was promoted to *SS-Standartenführer* on 21 June 1943. He subsequently commanded the division from 30 June to 10 July 1944. After this he returned to command his old regiment; then, on 2 November 1944 he was given command of the 25th SS Waffen Grenadier Division "*Hunyadi*" (Hungarian No. 1). At the end of 1944-beginning of 1945 he was placed in command of the 27th SS Volunteer Grenadier Division "*Langemarck*", and on 2 May 1945 he led the remnants of the division into captivity in the hands of the western allies.

28th SS Volunteer Grenadier Division "*Wallonien*"

According to SS Headquarters planning, *SS-Oberführer* Burk and later *SS-Oberführer* Heilmann were supposed to command the 28th SS Volunteer Grenadier Division "*Wallonien*" (Wallonian No. 1). Their biographies have been left out because *SS-Sturmbannführer* (later *SS-Obersturmbannführer*) Degrelle was the formation's only commander from February 1944 until the end of the war.

10/44 – 05/45 *SS-Obersturmführer* Degrelle

Léon Degrelle was born in Bouillon, Belgium, on 15 June 1906. After attending a Jesuit school he obtained a law degree. Between 1926 and 1929 he travelled to Mexico and reported on the civil war there. Inspired by the faith of the Mexican Catholics, in 1930 in Belgium he founded the Rexist movement, which was very close to the clergy. Following his rejection of democracy, however, there was a break with the Archbishop of Mecheln and Brussels. Because of this, after initial political success, in 1937 Degrelle lost a great deal of public sympathy. Although he figured prominently in the formation of the *Legion "Wallonie"*, he joined the Wallonian Infantry Battalion 373 as a simple soldier. Within two years he achieved the rank of *Oberleutnant*, and effective 1 June 1943 was taken into the *Waffen-SS* with the rank of *SS-Obersturmführer* (SS Volunteer Assault Brigade "*Wallonien*"). On 9 November 1943 he was promoted to *SS-Hauptsturmführer*. When the brigade's commander was killed on 13 February 1944, Degrelle assumed tactical command, and on 20 February 1944 he was awarded the Knight's Cross for his inspiring leadership during the breakout from the Cherkassy Pocket. Two months later he was promoted to *SS-Sturmbannführer*. On 27 August 1944, after the action in Estonia, Degrelle was awarded the Knight's Cross with Oak Leaves. Then, on 14 September he received the Close Combat Clasp in Gold. On 9 October he received the German Cross in Gold for his repeated acts of bravery. Degrelle was promoted to *SS-Obersturmbannführer* on 1 January 1945 and was named commanding officer of the 28th SS Volunteer Grenadier Division. He thus commanded the Wallonian SS volunteers from 13 February 1944 until the end of the war. Promotions to *SS-Standartenführer* or *SS-Oberführer* are not documented. When the war ended he fled to Spain, and in 1954 he became a Spanish citizen under the name Léon José Ramirez. Degrelle died in Malaga on 31 March 1994.

Recipients of High Decorations

27th SS Volunteer Grenadier Division "*Langemarck*"

Konrad Schellong was born in Dresden on 7 February 1910, and in 1932 joined the SA. After transferring to the SS at the end of the year, in 1934 he served in SS Special Detachment "*Sachsen*" (guard unit at the Sachsenburg concentration camp). Two years later (promoted to *SS-Untersturmführer* on 2 April 1936) he was transferred to the *SS Totenkopf Standarte "Oberbayern"* (guard unit at the Dachau concentration camp). One year later he was promoted to the rank of *SS-Obersturmführer*. In autumn 1939, by then an *SS-Hauptsturmführer*, he became commander of the 9th Company, *SS Totenkopf* Infantry Regiment 1 when the *SS Totenkopf* Division was formed. In August 1941 he commanded 9th Company, SS Infantry Regiment 1. Following a discussion with Himmler on 19 April 1942, Schellong took over the III Battalion of the Volunteer Legion "*Niederlande*" from *SS-Obersturmbannführer* Fitzhum. Promoted to *SS-Sturmbannführer* on 9 November 1942, from May 1943 he commanded the SS Volunteer Assault Brigade "*Langemarck*". On 19 October 1944, during formation of the 27th SS Volunteer Grenadier Division, he was named commander of SS Volunteer Grenadier Regiment 66. Schellong was promoted to *SS-Obersturmbannführer* on 9 November 1944. On 29 March 1944 he was decorated with the German Cross in Gold, and on 28 February 1945 received the Knight's Cross. He emigrated to the USA in 1957, however, in 1983 he was deported. While he had admitted being a member of the *Waffen-SS* in his visa application in 1956, he had failed to reveal that he had served in Death's Head units. Schellong died in Hamburg in 1992.

Remy Schrijnen was born in Kumtich, near Tienen in Flanders, on 24 December 1921. A member of the VNV, in 1941 he volunteered to work in Germany. In November 1942 he was recruited to serve in the Volunteer Legion "*Flandern*". Initially employed as a runner, Schrijnen later became a gunner on the 75-mm Pak 40 anti-tank gun. On 25 May 1944 he was awarded the Iron Cross, Second Class for destroying two Soviet T 34 tanks. About two months later, on the Narva Front, he knocked out three Stalin tanks and four T 34s and was awarded the Iron Cross, First Class. For the fact that he ultimately served the weapon alone and all of the company's other guns were destroyed, he was awarded the Knight's Cross on 21 September 1944. He was also promoted to *SS-Unterscharführer*. When the war ended he was captured by the Americans, who handed him over to the Belgian authorities. Released from prison in 1955, he moved to Germany. He died in Hagen on 27 July 2006.

In Estonia the battle group of the SS Volunteer Assault Brigade "*Wallonien*" was attached to Division Group Wagner. *SS-Brigadeführer* Wagner (on the left) was the commanding officer of the 4th SS Volunteer Brigade "*Nederland*". In the center is Leon Degrelle.

SS-Untersturmführer Leon Gillis was awarded the Knight's Cross for his actions on 30 September 1944. Note that Gillis is wearing the "*Wallonien*" cuff band.

28th SS Volunteer Grenadier Division "*Wallonien*"

Leon Degrelle (see biography under Division Commanders)

Leon Gillis was born in Courdinne, near Charleroi in Belgium, on 10 February 1913. After leaving school he initially became a mechanic. A member of the Rexists since 1938, in August 1941, at the age of 28, he joined the Legion "*Wallonie*". A year later he was badly wounded, and when Wallonian Infantry Battalion 373 was taken into the *Waffen-SS* he was still recovering from his wounds. Joining SS Assault Brigade "*Wallonien*" as an *SS-Oberscharführer*, he took over an anti-tank platoon. On 1 March 1944, after the breakout from the Cherkassy Pocket, Gillis was appointed *SS-Standartenjunker*, and on 20 April he was promoted to *SS-Untersturmführer*. He was awarded the Knight's Cross of the Iron Cross on 30 September 1944 for his actions in the Dorpat area. Three 75-mm Pak 40 anti-tank guns under his command repulsed repeated tank attacks by the Red Army. Finally, after all three guns had been knocked out, he destroyed three more enemy tanks with hand grenade clusters. After the war he was sentenced to 20 years in a labor camp in Belgium. Degrelle died in Vorst, near Brussels, on 24 March 1977.

Lucien Lippert was born in Arlon, Belgium, on 25 August 1913 and became a career soldier in the Belgian Army. When the Wallonian Infantry Battalion 373 was established he was taken into the Wehrmacht as an Oberleutnant and served as adjutant to the battalion commander. After promotion to *Hauptmann*, in June 1942 he assumed command of the battalion. After the Legion "*Wallonie*" was integrated into the *Waffen-SS* as SS Assault Brigade "*Wallonien*", on 1 June 1943 Lippert was promoted to *SS-Sturmbannführer*. He commanded the brigade until 13 February 1944, when he was killed in Nova Buda in the Cherkassy Pocket. Lippert was awarded the German Cross in Gold posthumously on 20 February 1944.

Jacque Leroy was born in Binche, Belgium, on 10 September 1924. He was supposedly awarded the Knight's Cross on 20 April 1945 as an *SS-Untersturmführer* and commander of the 1st Company, SS Volunteer Grenadier Regiment 69. This was confirmed to him by the former division adjutant in 1957 and his former division commander in 1973. No award application or memos concerning the awarding of the decoration from 1945 have come to light. Perhaps their intention was to honor Leroy after the war, for despite the loss of an eye and an arm he had boldly continued to serve in the front lines. In fact, it seems unlikely that he was awarded the decoration. Leroy died in Siegsdorf on 5 August 1996.

Military Postal Numbers

5th SS Panzer Division "*Wiking*"

Division Headquarters	16 284
SS Panzer Grenadier Regiment 9 "Germania"	30 003
I Battalion	33 576
II Battalion	30 629
III Battalion	34 002
SS Panzer Grenadier Regiment 10 "Westland"	25 854
I Battalion	26 907
II Battalion	27 026
III Battalion	28 109
SS Panzer Artillery Regiment 5	20 060
I Battalion	21 432
II Battalion	22 855
III Battalion	23 604
IV Battalion	24 976
SS Armored Anti-Aircraft Battalion 5	40 017
SS Panzer Regiment 5	58 040
I Battalion	08 158
II Battalion	57 084
SS Assault Gun Battalion 5	02 131
SS Armored Signals Battalion 5	33 631
SS Armored Reconnaissance Battalion 5	39 688
SS Anti-Tank Battalion 5	45 750
SS Armored Pioneer Battalion 5	44 189
SS Field Replacement Battalion 5	19 637

27th SS Volunteer Grenadier Division "*Langemarck*"

Division Headquarters	44 853
SS Military Police Squad 28	64 116
SS Volunteer Grenadier Regiment 66	04 206
I Battalion	64 485
II Battalion	17 662
SS Volunteer Grenadier Regiment 67	05 294
I Battalion	34 695
II Battalion	07 073

SS Volunteer Grenadier Regiment 68	64 712
I Battalion	04 336
II Battalion	65 078
SS-Division Fusilier Battalion 27	05 150
SS Anti-Tank Battalion 27	21 836
SS Volunteer Artillery Regiment 27	05 814
I Battalion	07 534
II Battalion	06 939
III Battalion	66 124
IV Battalion	07 944
SS Pioneer Battalion 27	66 467
SS Signals Battalion 27	44 853
SS Field Replacement Battalion 27	65 597
SS Supply Regiment 27	66 752
SS Administration Company 27	06 588
SS Veterinary Company 27	06 263
SS Medical Company 27	65 902
SS Field Post Office 27	66 997

28th SS Volunteer Grenadier Division "*Wallonien*"

Division Headquarters	38 918
SS Volunteer Grenadier Regiment 69	28 193
I Battalion	00 385
II Battalion	05 464
SS Volunteer Grenadier Regiment 70	16 821
I Battalion	01 379
II Battalion	06 974
SS Anti-Tank Battalion 28	43 857
SS Volunteer Artillery Regiment 28	02 544
I Battalion	02 544
II Battalion	65 856
SS Pioneer Battalion 28	36 637
SS Signals Battalion 28	44 853
SS Field Replacement Battalion 28	18 909
SS Administration Company 28	04 712
SS Motor Transport Company 28	38 714
SS Ordnance Company 28	41 461
SS Veterinary Company 28	18 909
SS Medical Company 28	03 277
SS Field Post Office 28	03 487

Speech by the Commander of SS Headquarters *SS-Obergruppenführer* Berger to *SS-Gruppenführer* in March 1944 concerning "*Germanic*" Volunteers

Berger's speech, which follows, shows how out of touch with reality large elements of the German command were. Berger's statements are a farce, as he must have been aware of the true facts. It is immaterial whether he was speaking about "*the defensive struggle to preserve [the] national existence*" or the enormous intake of "*Germanic volunteers*". For example, the figure of 1,812 Walloons included the approximately 700 members of the former Wallonian Infantry Battalion 373. His claim of a weekly intake of 2,000 volunteers had absolutely no basis in fact.

"*After the victories of 1939-40, the German people were presented with the opportunity to bring about a restructuring of Europe, to unite the Germanic peoples of our continent under our leadership, and to create a Germanic empire. Apart from Germany, there was no other nation on the mainland capable of carrying out this task. And so the focus of this war shifted under the influence of events. From the defensive struggle to preserve the national existence, Germany was obliged to go beyond its borders and defend all of Europe. All the more so, when, from month to month, it became clearer that, on the one hand, America was seeking war because the ruling Jewry there was not prepared under any circumstances to permit a rise and a concentration of European forces, and on the other side the threat of Bolshevism grew steadily. It was the intention of Bolshevism—as Lenin had predicted—to exploit the opportunity offered by the war in Europe as a laughing third party to achieve its objectives in Europe. This, however, meant the demise of all of western civilization. Our Führer Adolf Hitler foresaw this development clearly. For this reason he immediately released the Norwegian and Dutch troops in their homelands! He appealed to the National-Socialist forces in Norway, Holland and Flanders to work with Germany and gave Germanic men the opportunity to fight for Europe's freedom in the struggle against Bolshevism. Since 1929, when the Reichsführer-SS took it over, the Schutzstaffel has seen the Germanic empire as its long-range goal. This long-range goal must be offered if the SS is to have a unit of specifically Nordic men. It cannot stop before artificially drawn borders. Since early on, therefore, we have sought to establish contact with the renewal movements in the Germanic countries, and some representatives of these Germanic nations served in our SS-Standarten "Germania" and "Deutschland" before 1940. In the Führer order of 15 June 1940 it was established that Dutch would serve together in the SS-Standarte "Westland" as part of a Germanic-racial Reich policy. To ensure replacements for this SS-Standarte, in 1940 the Reichsführer-SS tasked me with the establishment of Waffen-SS replacement detachments in the Netherlands, in Flanders, and in Norway. The SS-Standarte "Westland" has been joined by the SS-Standarte "Nordland"*

On 31/1/1944 the state of volunteers from the Germanic nations was as follows:

Norway	*3,878*
Denmark (Danes)	*5,006*
Netherlands	*18,473*
Flanders	*5,033*
Wallonia	*1,812*
Sweden	*101*
Switzerland	*584*
Total:	*34,887*

There are also 2,480 volunteers from France, so that today we have a total of 37,367 volunteers in the ranks of the Waffen-SS. Weekly intake 2,000 men. The figure for Walloons does not include the volunteers transferred to the Waffen-SS when it took over the Legion "Wallonie"."

Tables of Organization

SS Assault Brigade (New Type)
(Authorized Strength approx. 2,000 men)

Brigade Headquarters
Grenadier Battalion (motorized) with 1st – 3rd Companies and
 4th (Heavy) Company
Heavy Battalion (motorized)
 5th (Infantry Gun) Company (2 light and 1 heavy platoons)
 6th (Anti-Tank) Company (1 50-mm anti-tank gun platoon and 2 75-mm anti-tank gun platoons)
 7th (Assault Gun) Battery (10 assault guns)
 8th (20-mm Flak) Battery
 9th (88-mm Flak) Battery
 10th (Supply) Company

Infantry Division 44
(Authorized Strength: 12,772 men)

Division Headquarters	227 men
3 Grenadier Regiments (2 battalions)	5,961 men
Artillery Regiment	2,013 men
I Battalion [1st – 3rd Batteries (105-mm light field howitzers)]	
II Battalion [4th – 6th Batteries (105-mm light field howitzers)]	
III Battalion [7th – 9th Batteries (105-mm light field howitzers)]	
IV Battalion [10th – 12th Batteries (150-mm heavy field howitzers)]	
Division Fusilier Battalion	708 men
3 fusilier companies (1 on bicycles)	
1 heavy fusilier company	
Anti-Tank Battalion	484 men
1 heavy company (12 75-mm guns, towed)	
1 assault gun battery (10 guns)	
1 anti-aircraft company (12 20-mm Flak, S.P.)	
Pioneer Battalion	620 men
2 pioneer companies (1 on bicycles)	
Signals Section	379 men
1 company (telephone)	
1 company (radio)	
Field Replacement Battalion	925 men
Supply Units	1,455 men
1 motor transport company	
1 workshop company	

1 supply company
1 bicycle troop
1 bakery company
1 butcher company
2 medical companies
1 ambulance company
1 veterinary company

Rank Comparisons

German Rank	Foreign Rank	Army
SS-Grenadier	Legions-Grenadier	Grenadier
SS-Sturmmann	Legions-Sturmmann	Gefreiter
SS-Rottenführer	Legions-Rottenführer	Obergefreiter
SS-Unterscharführer	Legions-Unterscharführer	Unteroffizier
SS-Scharführer	Legions-Scharführer	Unterfeldwebel
SS-Oberscharführer	Legions-Oberscharführer	Feldwebel
SS-Hauptscharführer	Legions-Hauptscharführer	Oberfeldwebel
SS-Untersturmführer	Legions-Untersturmführer	Leutnant
SS-Obersturmführer	Legions-Obersturmführer	Oberleutnant
SS-Hauptsturmführer	Legions-Hauptsturmführer	Hauptmann
SS-Sturmbannführer	Legions-Sturmbannführer	Major
SS-Obersturmbannführer	Legions-Obersturmbannführer	Oberstleutnant
SS-Standartenführer	Legions-Standartenführer	Oberst
SS-Oberführer	Legions-Oberführer	no comparable rank
SS-Brigadeführer	Legions-Brigadeführer	Generalmajor
SS-Obergruppenführer	Legions-SS-Obergruppenführer	General
SS-Oberstgruppenführer	--	Generaloberst

Bibliograpy

Forschungsstelle für Zeitgeschichte (Hrsg.): Dienstkalender Himmlers 1941/42, Hamburg 1999

Frießner, Hans: Verratene Schlachten, Hamburg 1956

Haupt, Werner: Heeresgruppe "Nord", Bad Nauheim 1966

Hausser, Paul: Soldaten wie andere auch, Osnabrück 1966

Heiber, Helmut (Hrsg.): Lagebesprechungen im Führerhauptquartier, München 1964

Klietmann Dr., Kurt-G.: Die *Waffen-SS*, Osnabrück 1965

Krätschmer, Ernst-Günther: Die Ritterkreuzträger der *Waffen-SS*, Preußisch Oldendorf 1982

Manstein von, Erich: Verlorene Siege, München 1979

Michaelis, Rolf: Die *Waffen-SS* - Mythos und Wirklichkeit. Berlin 2006

Michaelis, Rolf: Die Panzer-Divisionen der *Waffen-SS*, Berlin

Michaelis, Rolf: Die Grenadier-Divisionen der *Waffen-SS* (Band II), Erlangen 1995

Neulen, Hans Werner: An deutscher Seite, München 1985

Preradovich von, Nikolaus: Die Generale der *Waffen-SS*, Berg 1985

Reitlinger, Gerald: Die SS - Tragödie einer deutschen Epoche, München 1957

Schramm, Percy (Hrsg.): Kriegstagebuch des OKW, München 1982

Stein, Georg: Geschichte der *Waffen-SS*, Düsseldorf 1967

Steiner, Felix: Die Freiwilligen, Rosenheim 1992

Tieke, Wilhelm: Das Ende zwischen Oder und Elbe, Stuttgart 1994

Wagener, Carl: Heeresgruppe "Süd", Dorheim 1971

Wegner, Bernd: Hitlers Politische Soldaten, Paderborn 1982

ohne: Die Wehrmachtberichte 1939-1945, München 1985